Praise for *Left on Red*

"Bill Glynn has a unique ability to cut through the clutter and immediately identify what the key issues are facing businesses, executives, and entire industries, and solve them in real time. He can be brutally frank and about as subtle as a sledgehammer but it is impressive how many times he turns out to be right."

> —Thomas Tull, CEO, Legendary Pictures

"In all my years of doing business with some of the world's greatest leaders and most creative personalities, Billy Glynn is one of the smartest executives I've met. *Left on Red* is a manual for those who think differently."

> —Joel Katz, Media Icon

"Innovation is a way of life. To achieve it, companies must unlock the potential of their employees and surround themselves with thought leaders, allowing everyone to think differently."

> —Glenn Armstrong, VP Business Innovation,
> Amway

"Billy Glynn's *Left on Red* is exactly what America needs right now to accelerate change and innovation."

> —Tony Jeary, Strategic Facilitator and
> Coach to the World's Top CEOs

"Zone in. You don't want to miss a thing here, lose your head, or worse, risk being left behind."

> —Greg Ray, CEO, International Speakers Bureau

LEFT
ON
RED

LEFT
ON
RED

How to Ignite, Leverage, and Build Visionary Organizations

BILL GLYNN

WILEY

John Wiley & Sons, Inc.

Published by John Wiley & Sons, Inc., Hoboken, New Jersey
Published simultaneously in Canada

For general information on our other products and services or for technical support, please contact our Customer Care Department within the United States at (800) 762-2974, outside the United States at (317) 572-3993 or fax (317) 572-4002.

Wiley also publishes its books in a variety of electronic formats. Some content that appears in print may not be available in electronic books. For more information about Wiley products, visit our web site at www.wiley.com.

Library of Congress Cataloging-in-Publication Data:

Glynn, Bill, 1968–
    Left on red : how to ignite, leverage and build visionary organizations! /
Bill Glynn.
        p. cm.
    Includes bibliographical references and index.
    ISBN 978-0-470-23023-7 (cloth)
    1. Organizational effectiveness. 2. Leadership. 3. Success in business.
I. Title.
    HD58.9.G64 2008
    658.4'092—dc22
                                                        2008011994

Printed in the United States of America

10 9 8 7 6 5 4 3 2 1

CONTENTS

ACKNOWLEDGMENTS

Thank God for life's canvas that I am fortunate to paint on.

Most notably I honor my wife, Brittany, who has made my life worth living, and her family for their love and grace. My mom, father, and sister, relatives and the Sunday Morning Breakfast Club that helped me become who I am.

A special thanks goes out to so many who have inspired me over the years. Thank you so much, Thomas Tull, for everything. Joel Katz, Arthur Maxwell, David Argay, Jon Nieman, Barry Landis, Don Perry, Jay Allen and so many more I couldn't possibly name them all here, thanks to you, too.

This book would not have been possible without the maverick thinkers, excellent editors, and team at John Wiley & Sons. My personal thanks to Matt Holt and Jess Campilango for giving me a voice and Tammy Kling at The Writers Group for her collaboration in helping my words come alive on these pages.

FOREWORD

As the twentieth century ended, it was becoming clear that the old way of looking at the world and its business opportunities was no longer useful.

During the 1990s, a group of young entrepreneurs rewrote the rules for starting and growing companies. (Now, it is important to note that they didn't get every attempt right, so we saw many start-ups go down in flames. My take on their failure was that they had incomplete business DNA: lots of genetic material for great ideas but big gaps of missing "how to run a business" genetic code.)

From that seething sea of radical change, great companies appeared and are now worth billions and hundreds of billions of dollars. Here is just the short list: AOL, Amazon, eBay, and Yahoo!

Something else also changed during this time that is worth noting. Many of us remember the Jack Welch/GE era of success based on dominance in your market—first or second or get out. The trouble with Welch's philosophy is that it trained those who applied it to see the world in an ever tighter focus—creating a special kind of "tunnel vision" if you will.

Tunnel vision has a great short-term advantage because it keeps everyone concentrated on one thing. That gives an organization determined commitment and clarity of purpose. But that very advantage turns into a dangerous disadvantage in the long term. By looking at the future through a tube, these companies were blocked, by that same tube, from seeing an array of unintended consequences that were forming off to the sides. And, even worse, they could not see opportunities that they would have seen had they been in specific markets in even a marginal way. The inability to see those consequences and miss emerging markets was a direct result of tunnel vision—extreme focus on one thing!

As you read *Left on Red*, you will see the remedy for tunnel vision through Billy Glynn's stories and philosophy. It's what I call "funnel vision."

Think of a kind of "time funnel" situated in the present that extends into the future, narrow at first and then widening as it reaches into the future. You, as a leader, as an entrepreneur, sit in the present tense at the narrow end. Now, instead of having your vision constricted by a tunnel view, you can see a much wider array of alternatives in front of you. You see not just your strategic target in the center of your vision, but you can also see, surrounding your target, possible actions, events, and consequences that are unfolding as you lead your organization toward its vision.

With this wider perspective, you stay on target with what you had determined was valuable yet still see what is happening at the margins, at the edges.

Learning to look at your opportunities this way is one of the benefits of *Left on Red*. Where do the new great ideas come from? Billy Glynn will show you.

How did Microsoft miss Google? Billy Glynn will help you understand.

Billy Glynn has funnel vision in abundance. Every time I have conversed with Billy about an idea, he has almost immediately understood not just the value of the idea itself, but also the importance of the edges, the periphery of the idea. And, the cascade of consequences that comes with it.

This capacity—to see widely as you look toward the future—is invaluable if you want to start a new company, develop a new idea, lead a revolution.

Left on Red is a book about how to better see the business opportunities of the twenty-first century. It is filled with examples of the way Billy Glynn attacks an idea and explores its implications. What Billy has done with his book is given you a chance to see how his mind works. Again and again he offers insights into how you can see new opportunities and evaluate new opportunities that can form the basis for new businesses.

I will warn you that you may not agree with all of Billy's dictums. But that is not important. What is important is that he shares with you the sharp, incisive mentality of a twenty-first century entrepreneur. I am sure of this: You will learn things about starting a business you never knew before.

And that's worth its weight in gold.

Joel Barker
Futurist, Filmmaker, Inventor

The Visionary

GETTING IT

The grand play of life goes on—and you can contribute a verse. What will yours be? Who will remember you and what you have done?

On January 2, 1897, Ragnar Sohlman, a chemical engineer in his twenties, was shocked to read the published last will and testament of his employer, Alfred Nobel. Ragnar had worked in Nobel's laboratory in San Remo, Italy, for three years. His boss was Sweden's most famous visionary, a millionaire who had received patents for his groundbreaking invention of dynamite. Nobel produced dynamite on a large scale across the globe during an era of massive infrastructure development of tunnels, bridges, commercial buildings, ports, and railways, where extensive blasting was needed.

When Nobel died of a stroke on December 10, 1896, the world would soon learn that the great visionary left behind an idea as powerful and explosive as the product he became best known for in life. The world would also see that Alfred Nobel was a master at choosing Left on Red thinkers to work with him to bring his dream to reality.

When Nobel's last will and testament was published in newspapers across the world, his young protégé Ragnar was shocked to read: "As Executors of my testamentary dispositions, I hereby appoint Mr. Ragnar Sohlman, resident at Bofors, Värmland, and Mr. Rudolf Lilljequist, 31 Malmskillnadsgatan, Stockholm, and at Bengtsfors near Uddevalla."

The will read:

"The whole of my remaining realizable estate shall be dealt with in the following way: the capital, invested in safe securities by my executors, shall constitute a fund, the interest on which shall be annually distributed in the form of prizes to those who, during the preceding year, shall have conferred the greatest benefit on mankind."

This last clause caused great controversy among Nobel's family, the public, and even the government. No man of great wealth had ever done anything as bold and humanitarian before. The will was unprecedented, and no one knew how to execute his last wish.

THE VISIONARY

Nobel no doubt knew that only a visionary could change the world, which is why he chose the man he had mentored in life to execute his dream.

Visionaries see the unseen. They have an uncanny ability to bring wild dreams to fruition from the tiniest seedling. Visionaries are rare and rise up unexpectedly. Sometimes they create world-altering new products and movements, as did Nobel, Microsoft founder Bill Gates,

Apple founder Steve Jobs, and Google co-founder Sergey Brinn. Others are beaten down, victims of their circumstances or fiber, their great visions and ideas held dormant. Nobel was a controversial and forward thinker for his time. His ideas often caused conflict with governments and businesspeople who did not share his vision. But that never stopped him. In life, he changed the business model for development and infrastructure and building. In death, his vision produced positive social change for the world.

This chapter is about vision. It's about getting it and understanding what little corner of the world you want to occupy, conquer, or change. Call it breaking the mold, bending the rules, spinning the wheel of life, or taking a Left on Red, which is generally illegal in most states. The story of Nobel is compelling because it involves risk and reward, paddling upstream, a path less chosen, and most of all thinking in terms of tomorrow and how the memory of who you are will define your legacy.

The grand play of life goes on—and you can contribute a verse. What will yours be? Who will remember you and what you have done? Kind of gives you something to think about, doesn't it? Will you bide your time according to someone else's plan and schedule, or will you do something different?

THE RIGHT ON RED ORGANIZATION

I deal with entrepreneurs, misfits, and people with grandiose ideas that are often translated into businesses that change the world or at least a part of it! So forgive me for saying that most companies do not want to risk thinking and acting differently. They create cultures of process and order, building products and selling services from that foundation. They are Right on Red organizations, like the major airlines that follow one another down the competitive path year after year, concerned only with what Airline A is doing in the marketplace, instead of considering what *they* can do to effect real change. American makes a change to its cabin interior, and Delta does, too. Delta reduces its airfares in a specific market, and American responds with a competitive fare. Airlines A, B, and C spend more time watching what the others are doing than actually innovating. But every once in awhile a visionary comes along and changes the shape of the box.

When was the last time you heard of a U.S. airline offering in-flight massages like some of the foreign carriers do? Not to say it hasn't been done, or can't be done, or even should be done, but there's a lot to be said for unconventional entrepreneurs like Richard Branson and others like him who just cannot be confined.

LEFT ON RED ORGANIZATIONS

The breakthrough companies that effect world and social transformation are often like Nobel. They think differently and actively seek people who think differently. They are Apple, Google, Second Life, and social change organizations like Ashoka. Ashoka is an organization that envisions a world where *everyone is a changemaker*. A world that responds quickly and effectively to social challenges where each individual has the freedom, confidence, and societal support to address any social problem and drive change. Ashoka CEO Bill Drayton puts it this way: "Social entrepreneurs are not content just to give a fish or teach how to fish. They will not rest until they have revolutionized the fishing industry."

But where do these changemakers come from? Some are born, some are created by external life events branded on their souls. Nobel had been homeschooled with no traditional rules to follow. He was sheltered from the traditional educational system with its rows of desks and order and process, and it made no difference to him what had or hadn't been done before. This is often true for many entrepreneurs who create phenomenal ventures and businesses that make most people scratch their heads and wonder, "Why didn't I think of that?" To an individualist, the only thing that matters is what can be.

In the venture capitalist arena I see this all the time. Someone thinks of an idea, presents it, but doesn't have the courage or brains or street smarts or perseverance or ideation or network IQ to make it happen. And then, sometimes, along comes a person with all of those things, and more.

IF AT FIRST YOU DON'T SUCCEED

Thomas Edison invented a lot of things, most famously of course the lightbulb. Most people know that he failed several times before he succeeded, but he actually failed more than *one thousand times* to invent just that one product! Finally, somewhere along the way it worked—voilà! All of a sudden, who cares how many times he failed? The fact is he invented a lightbulb. Recently, there was an article that highlighted the richest, most successful, formerly bankrupt entrepreneurs, executives, and billionaires. The moral of the story? Try and try again. I've failed enough to know that when you're delivered a knockout punch you just have to get up again.

One of my biggest failures in business was an endeavor I refer to as BuildNOT though we actually named the company BuildNet, a business that evolved as a major league play to capture the building industry by storm. At first, it was the biggest and most amazing deal I had ever been a part of. Keith Brown, the CEO, was a true visionary with charisma, strong morals, and high intellect. We were the first ones in the deal and helped develop the business plan while building a top-shelf management team. Next came the first big merger with Fast—a large construction software business from General Electric. Soon the business took on a life of its own, acquiring more than 80 percent of the desktop and scheduling work flow software used by builders and a substantial part of that used in the suppliers' back offices. This meant if it rained and a jobsite had 40,000 parts spread all over a dirt lot and the builder needed to put them together again, the computers would notify vendors not to deliver more that day. It was a system of organization and inventory for builders. Also, because most builders work using the 80/20 Rule, they could directly order materials for the entire home and set up their critical path to manage everything from payments to work flow and subcontractors. Eighty percent of all homes that builders build are exactly the same, so the bill of materials can be auto-input and used over and over again as a standard. Only 20 percent are customized. This makes for a great use of the 80/20 model.

Now, the problem. Much of the business was leveraged with stock and debt to acquire other businesses. Some of us pushed the company into going public early to use investor funds to pay down debt, and we even raised $120 million for the deal, which, at that time, was the largest private raise in the region. But the senior team members made a tragic decision. They decided that building a deeply integrated back office tying all the systems together under one umbrella for the ultimate B to B system was the best way to use the $120 million, even though the business was doing more than $100 million in revenue at the time. But this tactic didn't make sense. Because we owned the supplier's back office and the builder's desktop, the model was ME to ME, and there was no urgency for B to B. Get it? They didn't.

By the time they filed a Form S-1 to go public, the bursting of the dot-com bubble closed the window on IPOs. A year earlier the company was massive. A year or so later it was winding down into bankruptcy. I would have made more than a hundred million dollars on that deal, but what can you do? You can't always hit 'em out of the park. The moral is to control your deals and businesses as long as you can. Bring in the best management, the best money, and the smartest people and make sure they all buy into a common vision. Or at the end of the day, some things might be out of your control and you might get a knockout punch.

It is a simple and basic fact that any visionary, no-box, Left-on-Red thinker living among us will sometimes fail and often be looked at cross-eyed. Sometimes their crazy antics will be ridiculed (think Branson, Bush, Trump) even while they are leading the pack. Whether you agree with them or not, being a visionary is hard to comprehend and difficult to capture. If it were easy, everyone would be doing it.

WHERE ARE ALL THE VISIONARIES?

For the most part, companies tend to hide, stifle, or tuck away visionaries in a dark room or in a cubicle. Only today's best of breed companies perpetually seek employee anomalies, regularly solicit ideation, and use every means necessary to improve their businesses. They seek and find dynamic new products and markets to develop by continually cultivating the intellectual base within their business.

Ultimately, these companies find ways to cultivate intrapreneurship, vision, and new ideas. They provide a business environment that promotes and influences innovation, keeps vision and imagination flowing freely, and supports failure and risk taking with tolerance. These are the companies that see the entire movie and not just one image or static point in time. Ideas are always flowing, changing, meandering, and cascading into new ideas and actions. Forward-thinking companies nurture visionaries.

If one goes a step further out onto the business branch, there is a distinction between forward-thinking organizations, large or small, and the next level: the breakthrough businesses.

Breakthrough businesses rarely become noticed until it is too late to play catch-up. These are the companies that are built by underrecognized visionaries that otherwise would have created the breakthroughs for some big company. As a venture capitalist who has seen a lot, it's been my experience that most breakthrough businesses begin as ideas in the heads of visionaries inside corporations, which they finally escape to start their own businesses. Often the results are so powerful that social change occurs, and the fabric of industries is torn and sewn back together to form new fashions. Many times, all of this happens when everyone else is asleep at the wheel. These are the companies with Venture Intelligence. They are big, bold, and fearless, and their leaders go beyond forward thinking. These are the people who live way outside the box—or never saw one to begin with. When these types of entrepreneurs lead organizations, the result is a culture emboldened to succeed with vision that's instilled in the fiber of everyone from the receptionist to the CEO. Most often, they influence and create an atmosphere that rewards taking a Left on Red without getting a ticket.

These companies have an *it* factor and an organizational DNA that acknowledges that the contingency plan may be better than the original, not just a substitute. Failure is just a way of discovering that something doesn't work. When Plan A doesn't pan out, these organizations find a way to ignite Plan B or C, and the contingency plan becomes a strategy for the future that thrives, dominates, and perhaps even changes the world.

TACTICAL TAKEAWAYS

- Plan B may be better than Plan A. Be open to it. Think big! Really big! If you're an intrapreneur, think differently and strive to bring new innovations to your organization.
- If you're an entrepreneur trying to start a big business do not settle for a small segment of the market—own the market. Use every resource you have and "perfume the pig" as we say. Get dressed up for the dance with management, a great board, great investors, great advisors, and most of all great PR.

- Leaders take note: If a visionary is paired with too many dream killers, his visions may lie stagnant. If a visionary is cultivated, his vision can change the world.

Insider's Viewpoint

Glenn Armstrong, VP Business Innovation Amway

Innovation is a way of life: This is an aspirational goal. To achieve this, companies must unlock the potential of their employees and surround themselves with thought leaders, allowing everyone to think differently and creating open cultures where innovation is celebrated.

It's the freedom to swing for the big bold ideas that transforms industries and businesses, and that kind of freedom and culture can't develop and spread like wildfire without a mandate from the top. It requires strong, dedicated leadership, an innovative mindset of always thinking and rethinking, and buy-in for all corners of the organization. That's the road to building a culture of innovation.

Amway posted $7.1 billion in sales in 2007, which was *12 percent more* than 2006. Thirty-nine of our 55 Amway markets posted sales increases with impressive results in Asia, Europe, and Latin America. It's a perfect example of a company built with an innovative spirit that has been able to link its heritage of innovation to execution and results, with the thread of legacy tying it all together.

Doug DeVos and Steve Van Andel run the business their fathers built back in the 1960s. The premise then and now is to help people live better lives, and significant family wealth has been given to children, hospitals, charities, education, and other nonprofit efforts, that will make a lasting legacy and impact on the world. In the end, that's what true innovation is about. Transformation to create businesses, products, services, and lives of abundance.

Amway is an organization that has been able to create a culture of oneness and a business of dedication to its people, with integrity. Doug and Steve have learned from their fathers, yet further enhanced their vision and corporate culture around entrepreneurship, constant change, and innovation. It is truly incredible to see a company sweeping the world and moving with such speed, while accepting all ideas and foresights without pride of ownership. Doors are literally always open. All employees are encouraged to think inside the box, outside the box, and with no box at all. My role is to guide a program of innovation that will build business opportunities for all Amway stakeholders, incubate and nurture new ideas, and to bring new ideas, services, and product to benefit consumer's lives. What a great opportunity.

Prior to coming to Amway, I was honored to work with Bill Wrigley, a fourth-generation Wrigley who inherited the company, and I saw legacy in action firsthand. Bill understood that innovation is what built the company, and it was innovation that would provide the path forward. He was focused on innovation,

(Continued)

and immediately constructed a beautiful functional building dedicated to it! It is the Global Innovation Center located on Goose Island in Chicago, a soaring glass innovation greenhouse with inspiring atriums and creative spaces to foster innovation. This center sparked innovative thought and action around the world. I've been fortunate to be involved in these great innovation efforts, and it's been amazing to witness large legacy companies with founders and family members who hold a true passion for the business and desire to influence and change people's lives for the better.

At Amway, our core products range from nutrition to cosmetics and from home care to water treatment. The quality of the products is exemplary and in supplements and skin care we have the best of nature and the best of science. With a high-quality team and family-oriented business ethic, we're focused on creating a winning innovation culture. This will get the entire organization involved and expand the thinking and actions beyond their comfort zones. And that's an integral part of legacy. Being willing to take a left on red by thinking differently, to innovating and bringing great ideas to fruition.

BUSINESS IS WAR

Business is war is a simple concept. Act or be acted upon.
Act or someone better armed, better prepared, with a
better plan will step right over the carcasses—even
yours—left rotting on the field of battle.

There's never been a more analogous way to describe the
landscape of business today than all-out war. War for
jobs. War for customers. War of ego. Man against man,
brother against brother, business against business, and
country against country. War is the biggest business there
is and the business of war and the application of its key
principles are astoundingly parallel when you overlay
military history on business.

Attila the Hun set out to take over the land and killed
everything in the way, with the exception of one. Why?
You may know the rest of the story. The Attila war strategy was to make sure that the story of this slaughter
would spread to the towns ahead on the campaign and
serve to warn the rest of the world about the horror to

come. Who would want to stand up to that? It was the same with Alexander the Great. Nations would lay down their arms rather than fight the monstrosity. The best businesses today draw from ancient strategists in their determination and commitment to dominate. Microsoft decimated Netscape. When the U.S. government sued Microsoft, it spotlighted the company's power and reinforced its strength. The government's action showed the world the behemoth that Microsoft was, and Microsoft had a business-is-war strategy that didn't include backing down. It may sound like a simple philosophy, but this approach sets apart those who desire to conquer and those who actually do (or, in proper business book speak, those who execute, compete with every tool in the shed, and win in the marketplace, and those who don't). If you are going to enter the fray, go big. Business is war and you cannot afford to be meek.

WAITING AT THE INTERSECTION

Companies that head down the traditional path and wait until the light turns green won't survive. In this flat, tipping point, techno-blog, iChat, YouTube, MySpace, what's-coming-next-world, business is war *now* more than at any other time in history. Things are changing. Fast. Entire industries are being transformed.

In my business it seems more than appropriate for venture capitalists and entrepreneurs to relate their experiences to military conflict and sports achievement. Playing sports, especially football, is like waging a miniscale war. We set up. One side attacks, one side defends. One team wins. With that in mind you have to ask yourself: Do you feel like a warrior out there on the playing field, passionate about what you do? Are you at the top of your game and committed to success every day? You'd better be, because the one who is most committed, wins.

The good news is that today in business, most executives fight with velvet gloves. That's an advantage for those of us who don't, because you can't win today with velvet gloves. People, companies, and sometimes governments come to me for advice on business deals and economic development and the ones who want a win-win for everyone might not be able to win. Sometimes it's a cutthroat fight and the winner takes all, and the win-win niceties get thrown right out the window! I tell them to be nice at home and be charming with their friends and family, but leave the niceties at home and play to win when it comes to making it happen in business. Be aggressive and committed and don't forget that it's a battlefield. When you forget, you get too comfortable.

BASIC TRAINING

"War rages in the hearts of men" is a timeless term attributed to Gita, that holds as true today as it did yesterday and will tomorrow. Eat or be eaten, kill or be killed, win or lose. Competition is fierce out there, and every day there are battles in our minds as well as on the battlefield of life. Those who don't believe it are probably in a forest hugging a tree somewhere! That said, it's also important to note that although the mean days of business still exist, a lot is changing. It's about transparency now, a free flow of ideas and connectivity with partners and customers in order to gain competitive advantages. You need freedom and the free flow exchange of ideas to foster innovation.

Sometimes I feel like a professional athlete because I get up every morning and go out to play in the major leagues of venture investing. At times it seems like war, but I'm passionate about what I do and know my career is tailor-made for me. Do you feel the same way about your business? Here is my interpretation of a passage from Robert X. Cringely's *Accidental Empires;* in it, the author outlines three type of people. Try to figure out which one you are.

1. The Commando—The commando is smart, fast, and lethal. The commando can single-handedly take on 100 infantry, cut lines of communication, and disrupt an enemy's infrastructure before ever being discovered. The commando sneaks in, in the dead of night and is out the next morning leaving a competitor on its head. In this case the commando is an entrepreneur who pulls a Pearl Harbor on an industry or competitor.

2. The Infantry—They follow commandos into battle. Once the enemy is disrupted the infantry can quickly come in and occupy. The occupying force can stabilize the landscape and put measures and controls in place to assure success and position the territory or the business to be successful. The infantry is analogous to the management team the VCs build to take a company to a public offering and beyond. This team prepares the company to grow and prosper under the guidance of the next wave—the Police Force.

3. The Police Force—maintains. The Police maintain the corporate culture, the balance sheet, and the long-term predictable growth of a large company,

private or public. The Police build and repair infrastructure. They put law and order in place and elect
political leaders to create stability. By the time police are in place the commando is long gone and
the infantry is pulling out. And by the way—
commandos and police never get along, hence,
why so many infantry and commandos who leave
the ship post an acquisition once their contractual
obligation is over.

I use this to point out the waves of building a company and the personalities necessary for success during
each phase. There's a direct correlation to military conflict. Who do you think you are? I'm a commando, for
sure, but all three personalities are important. Figure out
who you are and where you fit, if not for yourself for your
team and business partners. If you are accustomed to
sending in the shirts (the police) to fight a battle and the
competitor is a bunch of commandos—whoops—you're
dead! You won't get a second chance. Just ask competitors
about Microsoft, Cisco, Oracle, and Siebel, among
others.

BUSINESS WARFARE

When someone wants to sell his company or take a hot
idea to market I tell him to sprint fast and find the best
people. I think about that individual's mix of commandos,
infantry, and police.

If you think you are the best—great! We need mega-
lomaniacs to create vision and set lofty goals. But the organizations that catapult into success are committed to
the war of business and will do whatever it takes to get

the best talent money can buy on their technical and management teams. From an insider's view, hired guns work and work well, so hire the absolute best of breed. This is not horseshoes and you only get one shot. In business warfare, you can't afford to make serious missteps.

One of the most common mistakes people in business make is to continuously view the world through the lens of yesterday, failing to realize that tomorrow is fraught with ideas, relationships, and interdependent systems that govern our interaction with our markets and stakeholders that did not exist yesterday. In this sense we must view our business and the environment in which it operates as a living system.

The term *paradigm* is used to represent the prevailing set of rules used to interpret the current environment: business, social, geopolitical, or otherwise. Paradigms are generally set and interpreted as static rather than as constantly evolving. This is much like the difference between a snapshot, which gives us certain information at a specific time, and a real-time video, which shows a continuously evolving image. The benefits of the snapshot are that it gives us a set of conditions from which to consider multiple options and allows us to take a time-out debate and reconsider. The obvious drawback is that the longer we use it as our frame of reference the older and less valid the conditions are from which we are making decisions.

Joel Barker, the visionary and world-renowned thought leader, put it this way. "Funnel vision dramatically increases your ability to pick up both signals of danger and opportunity early enough to act on them."

Funnel vision helps you see the whole picture, which in turn makes your judgments more sophisticated. You can only make great long-term decisions when you have a broad view of the future. For leaders of any organization, the challenge is to make good decisions based upon the current paradigm while maintaining insight into conditions that suggest the emergence of the next paradigm. Good leaders and solid organizations have funnel vision.

Years ago I addressed a group of MBA students at Duke University and offered my prediction that America Online would merge with or buy CBS or Time Warner. It actually happened in 2001 and needed to at the time, but watch what happens next as AOL.com gets spun off—like Western Union spun off from First Data. In the past 20 years companies have aggregated all sorts of business, through junk bonds and buyouts in the 1980s to the Internet in the 1990s and early 2000. The next trend will be the debundling of companies in the United States—the taking private of big companies and the divestiture of companies where business is not being rewarded for being in multiple Standard Industrial Classification (SIC) codes.

This means companies are categorized into buckets like consumer products, durables, retail, and so forth, and are largely valued by a multiple of earnings relating to their stock prices. Companies that have absorbed many disparate parts and pieces are simply not rewarded for having various divisions or operating units in multiple markets or industries. It's all lumped together and while one SIC code is hot—say defense—others are cold, therefore the whole stock is only valued by one SIC.

A perfect example is Ball Packaging, which owns Ball Aerospace. The industry only looks at Ball Packaging as a CPG (Consumer Packaged Goods) company; if it had spun off Ball Aerospace (especially in the early Republican era) it would be more valuable than both companies packaged together. But this would have required a culture of visionary thinkers, or Left on Red leadership. It would be worth more in market capitalization, trading closer to a price to earnings (PE) ratio of 40 or 50 times than the old stodgy packaging business trading at 5 or 6 times. Avoiding missed opportunity and possessing the ability to recognize danger is a hallmark of the true visionary.

THE SCOREBOARD NEVER LIES

Playing sports is like waging a small-scale war.

We are all lucky that the playing field is even for the most part. Sometimes you've got your game on and sometimes not. That's a fact of life and true for most people. Ask yourself this: Are you prepared for battle? Have you done everything today in your power to make your business healthier, your mind sharper, and your life more worth living, or did you just change the channel again to watch that movie for the second or third time? Do it now before it's too late and the game is over. The scoreboard in life and business doesn't lie.

CHITCHAT

I've spent a lot of time reading about and analyzing people's lives. Hell, most of my life I have had two to four hours of sleep a night so I have had extra time to read up on all sorts of things. A veritable treasure trove of useless information, many would say—but like a lot of people, I wrap that information with business intelligence and take best of breed strategies and experience into my own life.

I recall having a discussion one day with my partner at the first venture fund I helped build. He noted the differences between my philosophy and his. He was a methodical thinker and a cautious planner while I was ready . . . shoot . . . and forget about aiming—just carpet bomb the hell out of them. Very different approaches of course, but it often takes different personalities working together to win a war.

In this case, we were just chatting about how to take a hill. He said that his approach would be to survey the hill—send out his scouts—coordinate his logistics, supplies, ammunition, and team, and when the time was right he would attack with everything he had! At the end of the day he would take the hill.

I agreed that it would be a good way to win and certainly a systematic approach even in business. My methods are far more radical but they work, too. In my partner's scenario, while he coordinates the attack, the defense reinforces its position and also occupies the high ground. At this point it will take up to 10 attacking troops for every defender (did you ever play Risk?). I look at things differently. I would spend all my resources in research and development, designing inventive ways to extinguish human life via nuclear, biological, and chemical weapons or any other means necessary. Once I had covertly developed my arsenal (and I would never enter a battle unless I already knew I could win) I'd politely ask the occupying force to leave the hill. The best business warriors are attuned to this strategy.

If there were no response? Time to act; and I assure you it wouldn't be pleasant, and it would be awfully disturbing to those who would want to fight the next battle. You see it wasn't about the hill, it was about using such massive force the first go-around that the next business or battle to fight is either never fought or the competitor fears you so much you gain the winning edge. This reputation building is a business tactic often used by battle hardened companies that have firepower, particularly those in Silicon Valley. Not a shot is fired in a specific market, but everyone vacates the land. Why? Because the competitors have heard that the rival is coming (for example, Microsoft said it was developing a product for a particular niche). Alexander the Great or Attila the Hun is on his way. I've seen it many times. Companies lay down their arms and leave a wide-open path for the army to walk in.

Are you committed to winning? Can you depend on the people around you to protect you and save your life? Will you jump out of the foxhole and charge into battle with your leaders and your team?

TACTICAL TAKEAWAYS

- The most committed win. Your competition is everywhere, but you may not know it.
- As soon as you come up with a new idea you'd better believe someone will be there within weeks with the same one and it is likely—especially in the Silicon Valley—to be better capitalized and have a great management team.
- Perseverance is critical and the key to commitment. It won't be easy and, if you're starting a business, there may be times you'll have to live without a safety net, with the house mortgaged, and life stretched thin. Business is war and war is ugly. If you do not have the right soldiers, the right ammunition, and the right strategy—you will get crushed.

Insider's Viewpoint

Mark Barry
Former Managing Director, Microsoft Emerging Business
Partner of OpenView Venture Partners

Today more than ever business is war. Companies have to constantly be on the offensive and that applies to emerging or venture backed companies more than any other. I have been engaged on the inside of a large corporation and externally as a venture capitalist and no matter what the opportunity the rules of engagement don't change.

Certainly my experience working on top of the emerging ventures group at Microsoft and across a $9 billion research and development organization enabled me to see innovation worldwide. It was a grand experience and also taught me about aggressive development and the culture of winning.

No matter what example of military history is used it is always up to the management team of large companies and small to understand what is at risk. This is their livelihood and opportunity for greatness, and only the strong will survive the battles that are imminent, with competitors, the market, and other large companies.

Looking at the Silicon Valley and worldwide venture and internal corporate innovation, leads me to believe the battles will only intensify and get bloodier. Left on Red thinkers are ready for a fight.

THE GREAT ESCAPE

3

Concertina is barbed wire wrapped elegantly in large, circular coils around the top of a prison compound. The coils are deadly, each one crafted of metal helixes shaped like screws, wound tight. It's not your typical barbed wire. If someone tries to launch over it, the metal screws jutting out pierce limbs and entangle a body, causing serious physical damage.

But to someone with nothing to lose, what's a little concertina? Murderer James Robert Thomas faced a life in prison sentence for raping and killing 81-year-old Jessie Roberts. Thomas decided that a lifetime behind bars was far worse than facing down the concertina and he planned an escape. He launched over the dangerous barbs along with kidnapper Willie Lee Hoffman, and both successfully fled the prison walls. Another escapee, convicted robber Nathan Washington, got stuck, ensnared in the concertina high above the compound.

In an article by Deroy Murdock about why prisoners escape, one jailer provided an explanation.

"There are always people who rebel against being contained," says Captain Dave Arnold, personnel director at the Virginia Peninsula Regional Jail in Williamsburg. "There are those who will take that to heart and make it their mission to get out."

A cubicle is a lot like concertina to maverick, individualistic thinkers. These are the ones who think differently and view themselves as prisoners inside the corporate walls. They will often risk anything to escape, even if it means going without a paycheck to fuel their entrepreneurial dreams. For these people there are no rules, and it's difficult for them to embrace the team concept. Every organization has rule breakers, and some of them are also very competent and effective innovators who need to be recognized and cultivated. These are the people who think differently and break the rules because they've found through life experience that their ideas were better than others most of the time. These are the brilliant thinkers who are used to getting things done better and possibly even faster without a team behind them. Are they team players? Maybe not. But maybe there's not always room on a team for them or value they can add surrounded by a team. In my experience these innovators generally do not play well with others. Leaders who harness these individualistic thinkers and shepherd them in the right direction instead of slapping their wrists for breaking the rules are onto something. This requires shifting the thought process from one of law and order and process itself being valued, to a mind-set and culture that embraces individuality, reevaluates the importance of teams, and brings those concepts together in a cohesive, well-orchestrated way.

Identifying people who think differently is critical for organizations that don't want to die on the vine, be whacked with a two-by-four, or simply stagnate. And once you've identified these mavericks, leading them is another thing entirely. In this new intellect-driven economy, the best companies recognize the value of recruiting highly creative types with emotional IQ, street smarts, and the ability to innovate. They might be part of your organization, but if you try to make them into team players, you may send them packing their suitcases for the next Greyhound bus right to your competitor.

The Left on Red thinkers are often the people who don't want to be led. It's important to understand how to bring them into the fold, communicate company objectives, and help them fit and contribute without making them feel like they have to fit in.

The authors of a 2007 *Harvard Business Review* article focused on leading "clever people," people of high intellect who think differently. They conducted more than 100 interviews with leaders and their clever people (maverick thinkers) at major organizations such as PricewaterhouseCoopers, Cisco Systems, Novartis, the BBC, and Roche. The authors summed up their findings as follows:

> The psychological relationships effective leaders have with their clever people are very different from the ones they have with traditional followers. Those relationships can be shaped by seven characteristics that clever people share: They know their worth—and they know you have to employ them if you want their tacit skills. They are organizationally savvy and will seek the company

context in which their interests are most gener-
ously funded. They ignore corporate hierarchy;
although intellectual status is important to them,
you can't lure them with promotions. They expect
instant access to top management, and if they
don't get it, they may think the organization
doesn't take their work seriously. They are plugged
into highly developed knowledge networks that
increase their value and make them more of a flight
risk. They have a low boredom threshold, so you
have to keep them challenged and committed.
They won't thank you—even when you're leading
them well. The trick is to act like a benevolent
guardian. To grant them the respect and recognition they demand, protect them from organizational rules and politics, and give them room to
pursue private efforts and even to fail. The payoff
will be a flourishing crop of creative minds that
will enrich your whole organization.

Understanding how to manage top talent is as important as finding these high achievers. You're not going to
lead an independent maverick the way you lead a con-
former or someone who prefers to follow. It's a myth that
all of those characteristics should be rolled up into one
person. You might have a brilliant brain surgeon with a
100 percent success rate excising deadly tumors, but he
has a bad bedside manner and doesn't play well with
others. Which is more important to the livelihood of your
hospital and the overall big picture? In the end, if you're
the patient you don't give a rat's booty whether your surgeon is a likeable, team player who sips wine off duty
with his colleagues and chats about their lives around the

water cooler. You only care if he is going to do his job better than anyone else on the planet when you're under the knife.

Left on Red thinkers have a value system installed in their hard drives at a very young age. They assimilate things differently and often develop superior cognitive reasoning skills. Most are very creative, intuitive, and street smart and use their intellect as well as emotional intelligence to think through problems and scenarios.

THE LEADERSHIP BRAIN

The brain of the risk taker and maverick thinker has been studied by various organizations and one study, published in *Scientific American*, revealed developmental distinctions in those who willingly embrace risk and think differently from others. The winning VC and entrepreneur can access the rubber band ball of neurological pathways and draw on multiple experiences and nuggets of knowledge to constantly change and meander through projects, while at the same time use emotional intelligence, the right and left sides of the brain, and general street smarts. Put all of it together and their aptitude and cognitive reasoning can rapidly simulate, calculate, and connect the dots, the people, and the deal from beginning to end in minutes. Now that's supercomputing.

Leadership comes in all shapes and sizes and changes over time, setting, and situation. We have all worked for leaders with vastly different leadership styles, from the autocratic and overbearing, insecure and manipulative, incompetent and indecisive to the refreshingly supportive, engaging, and collaborative. This brings to mind the ancient Chinese proverb, "If a man thinks he is leading others and turns to find no one following, he is simply taking a walk!"

Leadership expert John Maxwell says there are 21 laws of leadership. Others, like author and productivity consultant Denis Waitley might say that, among many other things, leadership requires perseverance through difficult times and rising to the occasion when needed. I personally believe that leadership is primal, like a lion chasing a gazelle. Studies of the animal kingdom show that animal leaders have higher levels of serotonin in their brains. Leaders in the animal kingdom show confidence, extreme vitality, and a compass pointed at group or individual survival. These primal leaders are wired with an instinct and a very intense, aggressive, and competitive nature from birth. The instinctual leader dominates. A monkey can be trained, sure. But in my observation, human beings are either wired to be leaders or born to be natural followers. If you don't believe me, take a true Left on Red thinker and try to make him a follower.

Of course there are specific tools and ways of thinking that can help contribute and develop leadership. This is an important distinction to make, because companies must endeavor to develop their people and stretch and grow them, even when leadership doesn't come naturally. Changing people's perceptions can make a visible difference in their lives and businesses and bring them closer to the psychological framework that comprises leadership, or even the venture capital and entrepreneurial mind-set.

The maverick, individualist, or Left on Red thinker sees and understands systems and human behaviors. He or she can see that systems are in place everywhere—in governments, corporations, society at large, and religious organizations. They understand that people occupy various roles within such systems in a hierarchy meant to subdue or otherwise assimilate skills into the greater system or to generally place controls around the masses. Most of the time it is necessary and vital to order and development, but that doesn't mean the mavericks have to operate within that same system, or even should. Left on Red thinkers see this for what it is: control. Most people feel in control but are actually conformists in a world dominated by a very small percentage of great thinkers, leaders, and a worldwide aristocracy.

Let's take a look at the laws of leadership and the multitude of books you can buy like *Who Moved My Cheese?* and *The One Minute Manager* among many others, and place them into a pile of rubbish. My theory is that if you have to read about how to be a leader you should go buy some Huggies Pull-Ups. Leadership comes naturally. Or it should, anyway. Improve on your life and skills but know where your limitations are. Many generations of leadership spawn good leaders but genetics doesn't dictate that it will be passed on generationally. Some people are good leaders, some are great, and some are so completely different that their ideas can change the world. Determine which one you are.

This book is not about throwing rocks at or peeing on the corporate hierarchy. It's about seeing things as they are and understanding how rules and regulations can stifle and smother ambitions and goals. This means it may be necessary to challenge the systems and people who are part of them—even at great risk—to truly rise above the masses and become a game maker as opposed to simply another piece on the chessboard of life.

Left on Right thinkers are game makers. They are not players of other people's games. This irony is evident in the MBA programs I visit and speak at, where the faculty is charged with trying to teach leadership. True leaders are born, remember? You can teach business, or management, but leadership? You can infuse leadership principles into people, and you can teach people how to manage others, but that instinctive ideation and planning and understanding of how puzzle piece A will connect with puzzle piece C or E is a rare and built-in "it factor" that cannot be taught. It's also important here to make the distinction between leaders and Left on Red leaders. The latter tend to resist other's teaching—unless they perceive it to have some merit or value. They naturally migrate in an opposite direction from the herd. They tend to believe strongly in themselves and take responsibility without fear.

I have found that in the start-up ventures that have brilliant ideation, the Left on Red leaders involved are superior in intellect and courage and show a high degree of aggression when necessary. They might even be ruthless beyond most people's standards, but they will do what is necessary when necessary to make a difference. Leaders make a path—they don't follow one.

TACTICAL TAKEAWAYS

- Every organization has rule breakers, and some of them are also very competent and effective innovators who need to be recognized and cultivated.
- Leading high intellect talent and changemakers means thinking differently yourself. Oftentimes there's not room on the team for a radical thinker, but there are always ways to manage to work together to add value for the team.

- Identifying people who think differently is critical for organizations that don't want to die on the vine, be whacked with a two-by-four or simply stagnate. Once you've identified them, leading them is another thing entirely.
- The new economy is intellect driven. The best companies recognize the value of recruiting highly creative types with emotional IQ and street smarts and the ability to innovate.

Insider's Viewpoint

Tim Wolf, CFO, Molson Coors Brewing Company

Leading a corporation is a challenge, particularly one like Molson Coors that inspires innovation as part of our DNA. It takes leadership that can manage today and see the future to cultivate individual thinkers and strong personalities and channel their ideas into action. To this end, we built an entire innovation segment within Molson Coors to extend a warm welcome to new ideas and foster innovation.

A Left on Red thinker may feel trapped inside a cubicle or the four walls of a corporation. Unfortunately, many ideas and great minds are stifled from reaching their full potential and benefiting the corporation. Our goal and Peter Coors' goal has always been to incubate ideas and harness our talent through a family culture and open-door policy at all levels.

Of particular note is the leadership brain. It is my belief that great leaders are born, and their brains

(Continued)

wired for high-speed thought. This is ideal for managing other clever minds.

Those that are born with the ability and vision to lead innovators are unique and not easy to find or develop. But the key to liberating the minds and spirits of the Left on Red thinkers in your organization is to allow the free flow of ideas in a structured environment to cultivate success. It's important to allow people to take risks and swing for the fences.

The Future

NOT NEW MEDIA—IT'S A NEW MEDIUM

Everything's changed. Nothing came across more clearly than that at a symposium of business leaders and industry giants called CEO Conversation that I host each year in North Carolina. When Richard Sarnoff, the president of Bertelsmann Digital Media Investments and executive vice president of Random House, stepped up to the podium and took the microphone, he opened the discussion up to questions from the audience.

"What's the biggest change in the media?" someone asked.

"One major change is the decline of the five o'clock news. No one watches it anymore. People get their news online or at the office, and by the time they get home they're ready to watch something entertaining. The second—commercials. The future of commercials is interactive. Like with *American Idol*, you'll vote for your favorite product and interact with what's being sold on your television screen."

Of course Richard knows a lot about the show *American Idol* and the power it's had with the consumer, because he owns properties much like it. The show is No. 1 in every country in the world, except Romania. Imagine that! No wonder why legendary deal maker Robert Siller-man bought it and combined it with his Mohammed Ali and Elvis Presley rights for real estate and attractions. The same types of cross promotion and brand multipliers that Richard was speaking about in April were being exe-cuted by Robert in June. Richard was on the mark and executing on his goal to transition from traditional media to digital media. That day in Raleigh he told the crowd that the new digital media convergence has four aspects: device, network, service, and the customer—all inte-grated and changing the way we interact, view, and buy.

The new buzzword seems to be new media. But the truth is, it's all the same media. It's the same as it was and always will be—artists creating movies, songs, books, and artwork. The media itself is television content, films, songs, poetry, drama, fiction, nonfiction, newspapers, you name it. So what's new about that? Over time the medium has changed—and it's the medium that has and will continue to cause huge ripples and a tear through the very fabric of the arts industry. Left on Red thinkers often see the changes happening across industries before others and position themselves to ride the wave as opposed to getting caught in a riptide. This is true in mediums and media, and we saw the Internet wave catch many sunning on the beach.

TIMES HAVE CHANGED

Do you remember the 8-track player? If you are under 35, probably not. Crazy, isn't it—it's a relic now, possibly suitable for a display in the Rock and Roll Hall of Fame. How about the cassette tapes or vinyl records? Dinosaurs and collectors' items. The CD and DVD are current but the videotape? Rapid changes are happening all around us not only in musical and movie formats but also in electronic media to deliver the content.

In the music industry, the cassette tape came out as a replacement for the 8-track. The fundamental recording technology remained but the form factor changed. Boom boxes and portable players came along and everyone was happy, especially the industry. Both the copyright side of the business and the actual physical record side were rolling in mud and money. Even the electronics folks had their iPod day in the sun—remember the Walkman and how popular that was in its day? What the heck happened there, Sony? A disaster waiting to happen. A two-by-four delivered by competitors.

Then someone had the brilliant idea for the CD. Exciting as it may be to revolutionize the business, it was terrifying to some leaders in the industry. It was sure to change the game and the game makers didn't want anything to disrupt the cash cow. Many record executives fought the introduction of the new medium, but what did I say about change? That's right. It happened regardless.

When the DVD got hot and MTV was in full swing the digital age in music and music/film had begun in a huge way. The labels, like the PC manufacturers, missed ownership opportunities in MTV, and Yahoo! and Google stepped in and used their platforms and media to create a massive business. And for sure, the radio stations never saw it coming, either. But despite some sour milk about that, everyone was making money, music was getting the support of video, and audiences all over the world began to see their artists, hear their artists, and feel touched directly by their artists in a way like never before. It was a revolutionary time in the industry with a lot of money rolling in.

Right again! Bam! Right over the head and a kick in the teeth. Along came Marc Andreessen, first with Mosaic, then Netscape, followed by a right hook from Bill Gates soon after. Like Windows for the PC, the World Wide Web put a face on the underlying architecture of what was ARPANET (built by the U.S. Department of Defense) and Telnet and became what we know as the Internet. The World Wide Web is its face and our Windows to the world. Hey, there's a new one—no wonder Microsoft stomped on Netscape.

So, who knew the Internet would change everything, change our world, open up new possibilities, both wonderful and horrifying? But to get right to the musical chairs game, when the music stopped there were no chairs. No one thought ahead, and the Internet became the game. Adults, kids, Grandma and Grandpa, Chinese, Arabs, Japanese, Europeans, Americans, and Latinos, everyone was in the game and the users were empowered to make their own online rules. That applied to music as well.

With the growth of the Internet, music became the central and highest profile industry under siege. Ouch. The Internet walloped the music industry and caught music executives flat-footed. Suddenly, instead of having to go buy music in stores people could download it for free. *Free!* The industry was about to be hit by a massive tsunami.

Change happened and the velocity of change was so overwhelming that the time it took the industry to react was devastating. What to do? This was a major issue for years. Still today, the digital rights management standards have not aligned.

A VIRTUAL SOCIETY

Who could have guessed how the world would change, from a plugged-in, hardwired, hard medium place, to an unplugged, footloose, and fancy-free one? Who would have guessed that everyone would have a cell phone and that billions of phones would be on around the clock?

The Internet can never be taken back. The music that was downloaded and pirated (well, stolen) can never be traced or recovered and now billed for. All the artists and music companies can say is, "Oh well, the band got a lot of exposure, and we will make it up in merchandise and concerts and everything else we will tell fans to buy." But with mobility, we can track the songs, videos, and the device via an electronic serial number (ESN). I helped Alltel and Lucent ventures in the early stages of developing their corporate funds and had insight into AT&T Ventures and MCI Ventures among many other telecom businesses, so I had a unique view of the mobility era to come. It was obvious that EIN, the phone identifier, was like a magic bullet. It was a solution because it was an activation code for the cellular device that allowed the device to be tracked. You can't track the Internet like you can track a cell phone.

iPOD, WALKMAN, WHAT'S NEXT?

Now everyone is in the game, from Nokia to T-Mobile to Motorola and everyone in between. Even the stodgy telcos and cable companies are getting on board. Today, embedded in a light wave, music is beamed in a second down to the iPod, PC, cell phone, or other device. This industry went from disembowelment to a diet and is gaining weight back now. But no doubt it got caught with its pants down for a moment—just another example of a two-by-four that was almost fatal. Lucky for the entertainment industry that regardless of the medium, content is King Kong.

TACTICAL TAKEAWAYS

- Disruption and radical shifts in culture inside industry and society are inevitable and always have consequences—many that are unintended.
- During the entire dot-com era "new media" has been a buzzword used by everyone. But the only thing that has changed is the medium.
- Content is information, and today it's coming at us faster than ever, in different forms.
- Content is still king and the major focus today is content—communications and commerce—what is it, how consumers consumer it, and how they pay for it. That's the bottom line.

An Insider's View

Joel Katz, Media Icon
Chair, Global Media & Entertainment Practice, Greenberg Traurig, Counsel and Member of the Recording Academy Television Committee, which Produces the Grammys

Over the years, I have seen the music industry go through its ups and downs. Music has had a forceful impact on our culture and can be measured throughout time as a fundamental characteristic of modern eras. Rock and roll, country, pop, and the blues have defined generations and have influenced and even molded much of who we are.

I have spoken many times on the changing mediums in the industry and the various forms music has taken. Regardless of how the consumer enjoys an artist's work—a song, a poem, movie, or story—it is the connection drawn and experience delivered by the artist that brings to life one's soul. It is here the value of the content cannot be traded for money and taken away and pirated. The music plays on in our hearts and minds long after we buy a song or hear it on the radio.

Watching the industry transform and introduce new mediums that deliver an artist's message has been a large part of my life's work. Without the fans, the money from selling music and the devices used to listen to it, the band cannot play on, the artists can't perform, and the industry can't deliver it to consumers.

5

WEB 5.0

In the 1990s, I was involved in mountains of captivating Web deals with worldwide implications, such as instant messaging and chat. Others broke new ground, like Red Storm Entertainment with Tom Clancy, Time Line Studios with Michael Crichton, and Interactive Magic with "Wild Bill" Stealy, which all had a huge impact on the way we would view and interact with media.

GAMES PEOPLE PLAY

Today, go into almost any home or store and you will see video games of all sorts. On TV there are dedicated gaming channels and movies being made from games like megahits Doom, Resident Evil, and a new one appearing in Hollywood soon based on the hugely popular World of WarCraft game. The crossover between gaming and Hollywood is a major breakthrough in the movie and game industries, because this cross-pollination stands to seed the economics of the target generation and fuel the future for the next decade and beyond. This cross-pollination captures and optimizes the loyalist and demographic. Who is going to grab Halo? It's already a mega game, and soon to be the next mega movie.

The games of today are rooted in the trailblazing of the past. Mitch Davis, for instance, the founder of Massive and now a partner in a $450 million game company called Brash Entertainment, patented the use of advertising in games. Bang—Microsoft snapped Massive up fast. Imagine the psychographic attention of children and adults when playing a cool game.

In the 1990s, when the game environment was taking off, the venture capital company my partners and I built quickly became a leader in the gaming space having taken Interactive Magic public and supporting the build out of Red Storm and other platforms.

Those companies brought new technology into the game environment. One technology improvement involved the latency that exists in the telecom infrastructure worldwide. When playing an online opponent, for instance, if you took a shot at someone it might take a second or two for it to register across the network if your counterpart was in Japan. Ah, a nice patent to have! We helped Interactive Magic acquire a small company in Grapevine, Texas, to get it, and the predicative algorithms allowed the online and multiplayer game environment to exist.

Red Storm and Time Line were both incubated out of a business called Virtus, which brought 3D animation to a whole new level. The technology that was the foundation of VRML (Virtual Reality Modeling Language) and had high-speed rendering on the fly at the processor level would change the look and feel of game play forever with high-resolution graphics and much more. Hats off to Virtus, truly a pioneer in the game space!

Kids today spend as much time in cyberspace and playing online games as they do watching television.

Digest that for a moment, and ponder the implications. If you really think about it, the television is starting to look like the 8-track cassette. On its way to extinction. Okay, perhaps that's a bit far off into the sunset because we all want to be entertained, but the 30-second spot is getting crushed, yet over on the other side there is a boatload of potential consumers playing games.

Gaming is an amazing way to bring brands to life before the eyes of the beholder. The ability to embed advertising into games and into television broadcasting and DVDs will forever change the way people buy and eventually crush the advertising industry's revenue from television. Right now we all see a 30-second spot, but it's not interactive. In the future, advertising will be embedded in the content itself so that when you're watching your favorite sitcom, for example, the ads will be embedded in that broadcast signal and you'll be able to buy certain items that you see on the screen by clicking a button on your remote. If you see a dress on your favorite character, you may be able to buy it right then and there. That's the advertising of the future. Interactive, here and now. Just like the Web, and what we've seen with eBay, blogs, Wikipedia, and other interactive communities driven by the consumer. Recently, Nielsen was persuaded by industry forces, broadcasters, and ad agencies not to follow its instincts and do polling of households and how often the families actually watched commercials. Smart move! You can imagine the results of that survey and how enlightening it would be for all those buying commercial air time only to realize that, unless there is a TV in the bathroom or kitchen—those commercials are hardly watched.

What's next? Advertising in your hand. Someday advertising via your handheld PDA will be something we all take for granted. Hit reply and win a free trip to Paris!

Think that's far-fetched? It's but a short distance off in the horizon. But for a moment, let's reminisce.

TELE VISION

Ah—the boob tube. Why are companies like Dell and Gateway selling widescreen televisions? It's because the PC architecture will be embedded in the e-TV soon. The software services we have today preloaded on PCs will soon be subscriptions and the features we order or use will be available on demand or rolled up into your service, like call waiting is today with your local television company's call waiting feature. The TV will be voice activated and respond only to the people it recognizes. The television will be able to handle your e-mails, letters, and bill paying.

One of the biggest advances in computing to come will be voice recognition and the computing intellect to respond not just based on math and a relational database of canned responses but to truly interact and learn from you and your preferences to serve your needs. The dawn of human-to-computer interaction is here, and 20 years from now I expect we will experience neurological- and chemical-based computing. Brave new world? Who knows? The brain-to-brain interaction based on individual brain frequency that transmits your thoughts and creates your mind's eye might be a species-level advancement. Sound far-fetched? What about cloning? Atomic energy? Stem cell research? We sit at the dawn of the molecular era. Nothing is far-fetched anymore. The advancements mankind will make in the next 25 years will dwarf all other innovations combined, especially in the area of human optimization and brain function augmentation.

THE POWERFUL AND INTERACTIVE FUTURE

The decline of the 30-second television spot has major implications for businesses, consumers, programming, and the advertising agencies. It has a cascade effect already being brought on by on-demand TV—digital recording and TiVo. The death is coming soon.

If people like my buddy Hamet Watt, who founded NextMedium, have their way, the TV will evolve into the medium where things are bought and sold, just like QVC and Home Shopping Network. Hamet was a partner in the New Africa Opportunity Fund, which invested $1 billion in the pan-African infrastructure to build radio, television, and wireless networks. He has been steadfast in his pursuit of interactive television, where product placement on television can be measured for effectiveness and managed and priced accordingly for its impact on consumer behavior. He's on the cutting edge of the future of interactive television and has built relationships with Nielsen and several product placement companies to secure a seat at the table when the real interactivity fun begins.

A few years ago, there was a lock on a 5-MHz band across the cable spectrum. The Federal Communications Commission held the spectrum for future usages but finally freed it up. This allowed an additional data feed to stream along with the broadcast signal. Soon, when you watch your show in the not-too-distant Web 5.0 world you will have power in your hand. With the click of A, B, or C—or a special button, perhaps a dollar sign!—the signal will pass in a millisecond through your television box and freeze that frame. The Picture in Picture (PIP) will play in a smaller window in the upper right-hand corner but that main screen will freeze. You'll be able to view the URLs for everything in

that frame—all the furniture, clothes, drinks, cars, jewelry—
yes, everything your fab favorites are wearing will be up for
sale right then, right when you want to buy. A group of girls
watching *Desperate Housewives* will be able to click on the
frame and grab that red cocktail dress the star of the show is
wearing, ordering it in time for her own party that Friday
night. You'll be able to order that stainless grill you see on
the segment of *Everybody Loves Raymond* with the click of a
remote. It's going to happen and soon.

In fact, it's already begun. Many cable companies use
the OpenTV platform with interactive commercials by
putting interactive options and buttons into the Ford ads
or Chrysler ads, for example. So when the Ford commercial ran on TV at some point "press XYZ now" would pop
up on the screen and the consumer could press the code
and receive more information in the mail or go to a web
site to purchase. The interactive game has begun!

Now OpenTV has sold its technology to 92 million
subscribers through its satellite and cable partners and
most people don't even know about it. The conditioning
and development of new habits is born to build in obso-
lescence. The world is being connected with new ways of
acting and buying. It is consumer behavior modification
on the ultimate subconscious level. You've already seen it
consciously via video on demand or an interactive option
in the hotel room. You've already purchased content
through your television via technology that's infiltrating
your home, and soon you'll be purchasing much more.

THE GOLDEN ERA

From virtual healthcare advice and doctor checkups through
telehealth nodes in the home, the world of information

technology has not even come close to its golden era. The Y2K and Enterprise Resource Planning era of the 1990s and the failed promises and scare tactics did drive technology to a more pervasive threshold than ever before. The crash was only a slight delay. The pieces and parts of the car—the muffler, the engine, and a few seats—were all sold to the company and consumer who could glue and bubble gum them together to make a system. Those days are over and the promise of Enterprise Resource Planning is yet to be realized. Improvements are around the bend.

In 1998, at an annual event I built and hosted at Duke University, I assembled a panel composed of representatives from SAP, Oracle, and Siebel, basically the leaders in the application service provider market. I railed them about the Y2K highway robbery and even embarrassed a few friends in the audience that day for being scared about Y2K. I jokingly asked them if they should get their money out of the bank. Why? Because Y2K was a farce! Imagine creating a story to make people spend trillions in fear of something that never happened. Fear is a powerful driver, especially in a technology-dependent world where consumers are wary of Internet fraud, identity theft, and a system meltdown. Not that these companies didn't do some things that mattered, but give me a break. A lot of businesses sold promises of a complete system but most were happy to sell the pieces and parts and let someone else figure it out—the CIO.

In the past decade, we've seen the rise of one of the biggest corporate influencers: the Chief Information Officer. The CIO. Corporations were so technology driven that they forgot about putting the customer and products first. The new mantra became *lead with technology* and it drove the American economy to new heights of efficiency. The CIO was an untouchable rock star. But many of the CEOs I know are pretty tight on control—freaks some of them, with good reason—and handing the reins of their business over to some techno geek wasn't going to sit well for long. And it didn't!

Yes, full circle. The world went from spending trillions on technology infrastructure to ripping it all out and handing the task over to outsourcing companies like Capgemini to manage. Forget dealing with all those wires and complaints, service calls and the jargon. Now watch how many businesses will smarten up and keep this trend going very hot for a long, long time.

INFORMATION UTILITY

We are at the beginning of the move toward the edge of the golden era of technology and information utility. I won't forget the time I sat with Joe Tucci, CEO of EMC, in Raleigh after he had just returned from a meeting with Jack Welch and Lou Gershner. It was apparent the gang had a vision of information utility that included storing information, delivering information, and billing for information. They would let ASPs, ISPs, CLECs, telcos, and data centers get built everywhere. All the infrastructure anyone could ever want. The railroad and automotive industries started with hundreds of companies and massive build outs and then consolidated. This would hold true for Internet services and infrastructure. The big boys would apply their war plan and war chest and simply gobble up and consolidate the whole industry. Content. Communications. Commerce. What are you sending? How does it get there? And how do you get paid for it?

Turn on the water and it runs. Flush the toilet and it empties. Turn on the light, pick up the phone, and bingo!

But from a consumer perspective buying a PC and connecting it in the home, or worse yet, trying to set up a wireless hub or DSL or cable connection? Better call in the Geek Squad. What kind of way is that to get people to use this stuff?

Soon technology will be plug and play out of the box, and it will be easy to connect all the electronics in your home. It will be your Microsoft home server. Just watch for all the new technology toys that will be coming your way! It will impact everything from your home security to the coffee maker.

JUST WHAT THE DOCTOR ORDERED

Technology will have an impact on the medical industry, as well. At least $3 billion is lost each year due to our noncompliance of medical prescriptions. When the doctor prescribes medication, we are supposed to take all of it and perhaps have several refills, but we often don't. I sometimes don't and I bet you sometimes don't follow the doctor's orders. Problem is, those money-making pharma machines want you to comply. And they want you to hurry up about it. Consume. Here it comes. Telehealth. Friends of mine for years have led the telehealth industry. It's the promise of a doc in a box, networked systems to deliver health care, with end point devices in the home and in remote locations and overseas. It's working and will revolutionize health care, early detection, and insurance rules. The game's a changing. Are you ready?

If you have diabetes, for instance, and today you sit home and don't exercise and you stuff your pie hole with junk, well, unfortunately that means you're a health risk and noncomplier. But soon you might be getting up, walking a mile on your treadmill, and then sticking your finger into a machine and possibly even speaking to a nurse over the home television, which, by the way, will soon have bidirectional cameras to enhance communications. If you don't comply and get your act under control, it's possible you will be uninsurable. Soon, the interactive technology will be everywhere—just turn on the faucet.

BACK TO FUN AND GAMES

It's not new media but new medium. Online gaming is huge. You can lose your identity in there, and lots of people do. In Second Life, you can create a second life, a whole new world for yourself. Online communities are allowing people to exchange ideas, money, products, and services in a variety of venues. You can even go online quite safely now via dating sites and meet, vet, and converse with potential companions you would otherwise meet in a bar or physical social setting. This will be mainstream and socially acceptable. This technology revolution has massive social implications, both positive and negative. But you can be who you want, do what you want, and play anything you want.

Coming up next in the 5.0 world are modified helmets and goggles and gloves. The new Nintendo Wii, an attempt to take back market share from Xbox and PlayStation (so far unsuccessfully) is using handheld wireless devices to simulate real action. That will look like child's play in the future. We are in the testing phases of controlling 3-D simulated environments that can integrate into your endocrine system and drop directly into your brain waves. Hey, you may think that's crazy and way out there, but you can bet it is coming! Your 3-D sight, sound, smell, taste, and touch will be approaching the real thing—think of the possibilities and the tragic consequences. In my forthcoming book, *RANT*, I plan to discuss more of the global implications and the weaponization of science. Regardless of the moral implications, we'll be blown away by the changes in every category of technology. What we know as consumers today will be changed massively and forever. Not just genomic medicine and interactivity linked to our brain activity, but even simple interactive TV and embedded advertising, and games so lifelike you will think you are really there. We'll have bidirectional interfaces for TV to TV communication—not just with the inferior experience a Webcam provides, but live and in full color!

BEYOND THE PLANET OF THE APES

Now let's keep going beyond stem cell research and the bionic man. Let's get into the human-to-computer interface—the melding of our flesh and blood with machine parts. "Have a heart" will have a whole new meaning. Already, scientists are merging human skin and parts with animals. These animal-human combinations are used for medical research and are called chimeras. On the technology front, look for countries like China to make some strange and questionable inroads involving human-to-machine processing. We in the United States may have ethical roadblocks but other countries may be able to forge ahead with human optimization and genetic engineering. We will interface our humanity with computers, which will create enhanced intellect, longer life spans, and major societal and cultural advancement and also lead to degradation and ethical complications never thought possible. The possibilities are boundless and the implications severe at a species level, if we do not keep our technological progress in check.

We can use wires and silicon to interface with the brain today. We can record activity and take pictures of it even. Soon, someone will be able to show your thoughts on TV, and trained psychotherapists will help you recall even the most difficult memories in order to remove them. Someday your grandchildren's grandchildren will be able to download the entire Library of Congress and every single language on earth into their brain and jack up the neurological pathway development 10,000-fold. Right now it's said that we use six percent of our brains. One day people will be able to access huge amounts of previously untapped gray matter.

The physics of your consciousness and neurological chemical-based computing is Web 10.0. Its impact on our species could be so profound and so unifying it would be as if we discovered extraterrestrial life that was intelligent. It could break down barriers and cultural differences and put everyone on earth at an educational level beyond our wildest dreams. It could spark a renaissance in human development. But of course there's a dark side: controlling and reading minds, weaponizing, killing through psychotic episodes delivered into a brain. It may be far out into the future but brain replication and organic science are coming. It may not be good or ethical, but changes we cannot comprehend are ahead. I have said it many times, we simply can not stop it.

As technologically advanced as we are today it seems that we are throwing rocks at the sun. We stand on the edge of scientific discovery the likes of which only God has seen, and I shudder to think of the possibilities.

As an entrepreneur who wants to go for it and capture the future, you have to be able to think differently. If you can't, don't force it. Fold up your tent if you cannot expand your mind enough to embrace the things that will be possible—the crazy, impossibilities of the future. Let someone else take a Left on Red, and continue doing your duty and contributing to the herd. The crazy ones, the misfits, as Apple likes to call them, know that everything that can be is beyond what exists today. Grasp the world of tomorrow and take its reins.

TACTICAL TAKEAWAYS

- The technology golden era has not yet arrived, but we are now at the dawn of the most dramatic technological renaissance in human history.
- In the past decade, we've seen the rise of the biggest corporate influencer: the chief information officer. The CIO. Watch for massive technology changes particularly in the areas of outsourcing and the CIO to become a manager of technology run by others.
- Technology will radically impact numerous industries worldwide—from medicine to media. It will be pervasive and out-of-the-box easy to use like a telephone or a faucet. The Information Utility Industry is coming and fast.
- The molecular age has begun and it is melding heavily with the information age to create never-before-conceived leaps in human optimization robotics, human and computing interfacing, and a myriad of future developments that will take us beyond the planet of the apes.

Insider's Viewpoint

Fritz Nelson
Executive Producer, Techweb TV
InformationWeek TechWeb CMP Technology

It may be tempting to predict the death of television with the huge popularity of Web video. YouTube is just the beginning. Companies like Joost and Babbelgum are not only trying to create a new viewing paradigm that adds an interactive overlay to your experience, they are encouraging entire new genres of original video content. Money is flooding to Web TV startups, many of which will discover and create new forms of information distribution, entertainment, and even advertising. These companies will take many left turns on red, and in short order the lines between traditional television and Web TV will blur.

There will also be interesting shifts in what we think of as normal television. The network executives see what the rest of us can see, and are forcing themselves to step up programming creativity by integrating the Internet community to drive their decisions. Movie executives are creating short-form video to use as content in order to promote upcoming movies.

So much is changing, it's hard to know what to look for next. Will Ferrell is spending gobs of time putting together video shorts and skits, just for the fun of it, but also because it's an interesting medium to play in. His YouTube videos have gotten a great deal of attention and views. It's also giving many others— the famous and the not-so-famous—plenty of ideas, and this form of experimentation will help uncover the next best ideas. No longer will we be tied to half-hour or hour-long formats.

All of this will mean great turmoil in advertising. What to do about the TiVo-nation we've become? How do you create short-form ad messages? How do you get noticed when programming is being produced in such high volume? There are good sides to this, though. For advertisers, it means having more choice over programming, more creative options, better selection of a target demographic. It will mean deeper experimentation with things like product placement and integration of brands within programming. Of course, some of this will also be doomed to failure, but often, these are the lessons that must be learned when turning left on red.

Finally, and perhaps most importantly for the future soul of our nation, this new world of Web TV is putting more power into the hands of the people. Citizen journalism is, undoubtedly on the rise and playing a vital part in the creation of news. Video has become a big part of this. Sure, ultimately people will value well-thought-through content experiences, with high-quality video, the right camera angles, well-lit scenes and the rest of it. But they also want something authentic and real, and now they can get it. Who knows what changes this will bring.

6

WEAINTGOTSH#%.COM

Elaine Gazzarelli became famous for predicting the huge stock market crash of 1986. In 1999, at the height of the Internet fever, I went out and bought the URL weaintgotshit.com (pardon my French), to illustrate the market we were seeing. I don't have a crystal ball, but I am smart enough and cynical enough to know something is a complete sham and a mockery of one's intellect when Pets.com, Toys.com, or just about anything dot-com had megamillions invested and megabillion-dollar market caps.

Money was ripped out of the day trader's pockets, re-tirees' accounts, and pensions plans worldwide to fuel the stock of companies private and public that had absolutely ridiculous business plans. A whole bunch of nothing, complete crap, and even I was a venture capitalist smack dab in the middle of the bush—shooting blanks at the enemy. By 2001 the money was gone. More than a tril-lion dollars lost in the blink of an eye. So much poop, hype, and bull. The world was up to its eyeballs in it. Some decided to jump off a high bridge just because they were told to do so and the stock was hot and coming back big-time.

I remember being on tech TV about this time. My partners were so nervous about my appearance that they flew out to San Francisco to watch over me and hover around while I bantered back and forth with the Forbes writer, a Silicon Valley icon known for the Sun Microsystems investment, and a retail guru. Whoop-dedo! What was all the fuss about? I was on the board of *Upside* magazine with the well-known Tim Draper and Dixon Doll and used to the public spotlight.

I wondered, what's so special about Tech TV and John Dvorak?

It was time for the questions, which we received in the Green Room. I must have been like Charlie Brown and got a rock for Halloween or something because I didn't read this question on my card.

"Bill," Dvorak said, "isn't it true that venture capitalists made so much money during all the Internet hype and propelled their companies into lofty positions in the markets, all the while promoting, selling, and hyping their businesses—only to pull their money out early and take massive profits?"

I thought I'd had a hardball thrown at me by Chris Matthews or Bill O'Reilly. I was called out. Nice!

"Yes, John," I said, "certainly true, the venture folks made a lot of money. A whole lot. The day traders and pension folks and even Grandma did, too. But when the music stopped playing and there weren't many chairs to sit in, everyone hit the floor. And while everyone was making money, no one complained. So now the bubble burst and everyone is pointing fingers and perhaps at the venture capitalists—after all they are *making it happen*. But one thing to note—everything anyone ever heard, ever read, ever saw came from people like you, John—the media. Right?"

A good story to tell but all the same repulsive. So many became so rich and many who became rich went bankrupt—some stayed alive and some became billionaires. History will call them, or at least I will be the first to, the robber barons of the 1990s, glorified for their wealth and power, gaining prestige every moment their stock value and personal net worth rose another billion. What happened? Was this the pillage of the American public, the global investor, or just another cycle like the biotech bubble in the early 1990s? I'd say a bit of both although this time the advent of the unregulated, under-educated day trader crept into the market and really created a thrill ride—a new demand input into the economic equation of market making for stock.

VENTURE INTELLIGENCE

During the 1980s and 1990s, well over a trillion dollars was driven into the economy to support innovation in the United States. In the early 1990s when the bio-tech bubble burst, major corporations purged R & D and pushed scientific prowess into the entrepreneurial world. Throughout that decade, massive inflows of venture capital and corporate posturing drove market innovation to a historical high. Boom! That, too, blew up. There was a huge vacuum in the U.S. economy sure to be filled by entrepreneurs, universities, and venture capitalists wanting to cement a lasting partnership with major corporations that would acquire applied research—in lieu of funding it entirely on their balance sheets. This held true once the monster companies of the information age—Cisco, eBay, Amazon, Oracle, Microsoft, and so on, solidified their go-to-market dominance.

The United States has changed from an agrarian and manufacturing-based economy to an innovation economy. The United States' economic place in the world is tied to intellectual property and creativity that the rest of the world manufactures and consumes. This is not to say we won't eat the dog food, too, and even produce some; however, the United States simply cannot compete in many old economy industries any longer. Instead of the pontification in the media over lost jobs, we'd be better focused on changing the system to retool our workforce as a nation and *enhance* our systems of education, exploration, and exploitation of ideas. People in your corporate culture or beside you in the trenches don't just think differently without someone encouraging them to. You have to guide them and inspire them to go large, or go home, to take risks in order to reap the rewards. Here's the secret: Left on Red thinking can change things, but it has to be cultivated.

A NEW WORLD ORDER

The steam engine, airplane, automobile, atomic energy, the genome, the Internet. American innovation has changed the world. In the realm of globalization, the world is an engine and each part of it an integral functioning mechanism. The United States has evolved from an engine itself to creating and supplying the fuel for the engine, and this evolution is more than just a fleeting moment in time.

The trends represent an underlying cycle driven by the very heart of the U.S. economy. As the global economy continues to mature, the United States faces an economic identity crisis. Can America retool its economic, social, and educational infrastructure to keep pace with its own value proposition to the world? Do we even recognize it? If we do how can we—you and I—see it, learn about it, and use methods and tools to win?

I watched firsthand the Linux explosion when Red Hat took off about five miles from my venture capital business in North Carolina. The incoming CEO, an acquaintance, had been at a few businesses in the area, and I remember clearly the day he jumped right off a bridge with no safety net and took on King Kong. That war still rages on.

Another industry that got crushed because it forgot to go big and develop a strategy for survival is the PC industry. PC manufacturers got killed by AOL, Google, Yahoo!, eBay, and nearly every online company until nearly every online company devolved the computer into a commodity and it never became what it should have—a point-of-sale device. If it had, it would have allowed computer companies to control consumer access to the Internet and the e-commerce to follow.

It simply became a low margin business selling the hardware that is necessary to enter the cyber world, and they left all their chips on the table while cyber world giants became billion dollar companies. How's that for a stick right in the a—I mean eye. Makes you wonder why no one asked them why they let all those companies grow up riding on their shoulders.

Could that happen to you in your business? It's time to start thinking.

HISTORY REPEATS!

The Romans and Visigoths, Marie Antoinette, the American Revolution, the Russian Revolution, the railroad, the automotive industry, telecom, biotech, Internet, all suffered and bubbles burst. And we all know how history repeats itself. Massive build-out in hundreds of companies, huge wealth creation, transfer of wealth, irrational exuberance, market crashes, liquidity crunches, digestive issues, bankruptcy, consolidation, aggregators, winners and losers.

The difference today from the Roaring Twenties and the post-World War II boom, the depression and recession, savings and loan and junk bond scandal, or corporate crime is that the cycles mentioned above are massively compressed. What took 30 years before to develop, contract, and consolidate into the big three, for example, is happening in shock waves lasting one to five years. The speed of innovation and adoption and worldwide domination happens so fast that not even the creators have a complete handle on it.

Countries may take our ideas, manufacture our goods and even buy them, too, but they can never replicate the American innovation engine pumping the world's manufacturing and production facilities full of intellectual fuel.

Today, still reeling from losses caused largely by the tech market crash, R & D across the board has been downsized. Corporate labs and venture groups have been purged and are just now getting back into the game. In 2000–2001, corporate investing and corporate venture capital was 17 percent of the entire private equity market. By the end of 2001 it was 2 percent. Today, it's back to around 8 or 9 percent. Still, it's no revelation that innovation has always provided the lever of vast wealth creation, of increasing economic productivity, employment, and wage growth, health care advances; the very economic wealth and longevity that every CEO desperately needs in order to earn the right to lead.

We are in an age where clock rate and tech speed are used to describe the market; where ideas are time sensitive and ecosystem metaphors are the best way to understand marketplace relationships. In this environment, innovation is the mandate and the Left on Red companies are the ones rethinking the formula for marketplace viability and sustainable success.

TACTICAL TAKEAWAYS

- History repeats. You just don't want it repeating on you.
- The U.S. economy is suffering from an identity crisis as it has become the intellectual fuel driving the world's manufacturing and production engines. Economies in the East, like China and India, are going to be of equal or even greater strength in the twenty-first century. Understand this and be prepared for the inevitable changes.
- The economy is past the bubble now and in a fragile recovery. It is time we and our leaders stood up and stood out for change, social and political.

Insider's Viewpoint

Arthur Maxwell, Founder, AIS
Venture Capitalist and Renowned Deal Maker
Recognized as One of the Nation's Top Operators

Having been an investor in venture funds, venture-backed companies, entrepreneurial businesses, and

(Continued)

large pools of capital, I have sat on every side of the table in the transactional world of finance and venture capital. I hope I can offer some wisdom to the entrepreneurs and innovators reading Bill's book. First, be authentic. Make sure you are real and don't overstate anything. Investors are tolerant but not of BS. Secondly, if an investor who has been in many deals before offers advice, take it! Sometimes advice is more valuable than money.

Innovation is changing. I personally managed a pool of capital worth more than $1 billion from the Middle East. After 9/11 I returned the capital. Although it was a great time to invest and do deals, it dawned on me the world was shifting radically. This is going to continue and the twenty-first century won't be dominated by American policy or economics. America will be the center for ideation venture capital and worldwide innovation. But we will have to subordinate our feeling of entitlement to hang on to legacy businesses like agriculture and manufacturing and allow that to be done elsewhere. There is much change abounding on the world stage, and I am hopeful we will see America be nimble enough to change positively toward its new role in the world economy.

III

The Art of a Deal

DEAL DU JOUR

Every day is a new day in venture capital —a new deal to work on, new people to meet, and new deals to be birthed. It's an amazing universe, yet of the thousands of deals VCs look at in a year perhaps only 5 or 10 will get funded. That's the sober truth.

"Buy me the biggest goose in all of London!" Everyone wants a VC to throw down the magic quarter and bestow merry wishes upon their company with millions of dollars, but frankly there are many hurdles to getting funded. I have been an investor, entrepreneur, and an institutional investor in venture capital funds. I've also created my own, and in every case, have relied on the value of relationships to leverage a deal.

The venture industry is largely about relationships and referrals. If a partner's corporate lawyer, CPA, successful entrepreneur, or otherwise big swinger doesn't introduce you, then your deal is likely to go right to the bottom of the pile on an analyst's desk. In venture deals it is important to deal as high as possible on the totem pole to get things done. Deal with a managing director or principal because the venture firm is run by its partners and only the partners can make investment decisions.

Many of the partners can make their own decisions and allocate monies but most have to like a deal, like you, and like the business! Next step is to have them champion it internally while every partner's bladder is relieved on it. Seriously, they'll be shooting holes in it and trying to find reasons to shoot it down. If it hasn't been flushed or put into file 13 then you have a chance! Now for the positive side of things.

TERM SHEET

Yes, the term sheet. It is a coveted piece of paper that lays out the general parameters under which an interested VC will be willing to make an investment. It guides you through the specific instrument they would like to use to invest with (participating preferred stock, convertible preferred stock, senior or subordinated debt, and so on). The term sheet will also include many other issues related to change of control, board seat, or observation rights, put options, liquidation preferences, and so on. The term sheet is only the beginning of the courtship. It is like being asked out on a date.

Now the fun begins. Most entrepreneurs at this point are thrilled unless the term sheet is harsh. Take eBay for example. Benchmark Capital gave eBay a ridiculous loan of somewhere around $500,000 and took a huge chunk of stock for the deal. In the end who cares? Both made billions but imagine turning a few hundred thousand into billions. This happens often in the venture universe. The results aren't always the same, but the term sheet is only the beginning of the relationship!

THE DEAL OF THE DAY

The best of all worlds for many venture capitalists is that you have no option but their money. For the entrepreneur, the key is having multiple options and term sheets. In that scenario, the value of the business (which is usually some arbitrary number plucked out of someone's behind) can be better maintained because there is competition for the deal. Smart entrepreneurs watch out for standstill provisions, which means that they cannot show a deal to other investors and potential investors while the VC they are working with completes his process on the deal. The worst thing you can ever do is go through this process without any money and with very little money to get you through.

NEGOTIATING A TERM SHEET

If you're an inventor or entrepreneur with a fascinating idea, this chapter is for you. Before you run out and sign a term sheet make sure you consult a deal making attorney. In fact, before you even start your deal get one of these guys or gals on board because that is your entrée into the venture capital world. While you may or may not be happy with the terms of the deal, the form the investment will take, the rights they are asking for, oversight, or management changes, you still have a chance to call off the date or simply change the time and place to meet. In other words, this may be a hot date and you are anxious to get going, but keep it in your pants and let the lawyers protect your interest while working pleasantly with your potential partner to iron out details and negotiate some terms. If the VC really likes your deal and likes you he will likely be a bit flexible about moving things around.

DUE DILIGENCE

Proctology 101. You better be who you say you are and have what you claim you have and everything better be documented tightly. Potential entrepreneurs building a business and pitching to a VC had better have reviewed everything and have professional consultation from a CPA and a lawyer to make sure the whole ship is clean as a whistle. People who want the money and want to convince the VCs that they know what they are doing and already know their expectations, often hire professionals to represent them. The best way to go into a meeting with a venture capitalist directly or with a professional is to prepare a due diligence book containing articles of incorporation, every contract and employment agreement, the capital structure and stock ownership of the deal, all the minutes of the board meetings, financials audited going back and projected going forward, and more. The ones who win have this ready. Their information is already tabulated and organized, making it easier for the VCs to understand and embrace.

YIKES! THE TERM SHEET AGAIN

The way in which a new venture will pass due diligence and get through the scrutiny will either enhance and improve standing or erode negotiating position. Conditions will be set forth in another document and this one will be binding—the prenuptial agreement, so to speak.

Documents are referred to as docs. Lawyers make a bunch of money proving their value through iteration after iteration of fine print changes on docs, and draft after draft and red line and blue line changes and more negotiation of fine points. This is painful but necessary. So when the documents are complete and the terms agreed upon and everyone is still singing "Kumbaya," then away we go and get married, and believe me you do not want to try to divorce a venture capitalist! Thus, the prenuptial documents are important.

A BAD DEAL

All entrepreneurs have observed bad deals at one point or another. I was once part of a deal that turned sour, and the company conveyed in all the due diligence numbers and use of proceeds (the investment) things that simply were not true. Thirty days later, the company had already run out of money.

After anxiety and panic attacks and a bunch of all-nighters the deal actually got what's called "worked out." This means that you have to accept the crap hand you have and get the deal straightened out and get rid of the filthy thing fast and try to recover your money.

CONTRA DEAL

Ask any VC what his or her "contra portfolio" looks like and they will surely laugh. This is the portfolio of investments the VC looked at and never did. I have a good one that ends with a kick in the pants. David (as I'll call him here) and his partner Terry had what I thought was a great deal in the cable space. David, the quintessential entrepreneur, and Terry, the technical guru, had developed a technology I thought was going to have a huge impact in the cable and cable modem space. I loved it and wanted to do the deal. My partner loved it, too. As it turned out, after so many questions and answers from our side and term sheets back and forth back and forth, the partners on our team just couldn't get comfortable with the deal. Well, it sure wasn't comfortable to learn that about a year later David, who had been almost bankrupt at the time, had a 30,000 square foot house, cars out the wazoo, and a hundred million dollars in the bank. Terry graciously came to speak at our Upside Event at Duke University the following year. As he came off stage after a speech I said, "Hey, congrats on your deal!"

He replied, "Oh yeah, you were going to put $500,000 into our deal and you would have made $50 million," and he proceeded to walk by.

Ouch! How's that for a kick in the shorts?

A home run is a deal that's a win-win for everyone.

Look at Tim Sanders, the author of "Love Cat," who was instrumental in the success of Mark Cuban's Broadcast.com. I didn't buy a lottery ticket, either, so don't feel bad. I also didn't build Broadcast.com and sell it to Yahoo! for a truckload of goodies and then go on to buy the Dallas Mavericks. Those deals happen! People make billions and people lose billions. Schoolteachers, regular guys, former executives. Unless you are on the inside of the industry and have the various deals and platforms to build and merge companies that are being invested in together it's a crapshoot and you are like a day trader playing craps at a casino. Sometimes it's already rigged and sometimes the players just get darn lucky.

ANATOMY

So let's step back from the clouds for a minute. As far as deals go, everyone has been squawking for years now about digital rights management or DRM. You would think by this time Verisign would have figured out how to handle all this for the music and film industry, but everyone was too busy acquiring each other and worrying about the blowup of the record industry and soon the video industry to stop and figure out how to get the genie back in the bottle. Well, it is finally happening. Although the record side of the business is gone, just wait and see what the buyout guys will make EMI do digitally.

Secure Path is a small company in Los Angeles that was founded by a few guys out of the film and finance world. Their goal was to become the dominant registration agent for the ISAN (International Standard Audiovisual Number), which is a voluntary numbering system for the identification of audiovisual works. It provides a unique, internationally recognized, and permanent reference number for each audiovisual work registered in the ISAN system.

To become the agent in North America would take money, time (which no one has), and a big leap of faith from investors. The investors came in early, and they were the same ones who came in early in WebMD and made quite a return! They saw the vision and my job was to take the deal after the money was plowed in and spin gold out of hay.

The team was superior and attracted great talent right away. They got all seven of the major studios. All they needed now was big technology partners. I helped connect the dots and brought the deal to First Data, at the time the largest credit and debit card issuer in the world and the world's largest transaction processing and clearinghouse, and to Global Exchange, representing more than 175,000 manufacturers and retailers.

After a bit of time and research it was evident that Global Exchange could take the registry that Secure Path wanted to build and crank it out globally. It could track every piece and part of the digital media no matter where it went or how it got there. I brought in a crack team of developers, "near shore" as we call it—some here on-site in the United States and some overseas in India—that got the system built under the guidance of Securepath's hot-shot CTO. It was hooked up with Oracle and Microsoft, too, but I brought in the bigger monkeys there to move the deal along. All in all it was a great deal. Isn't it great when things work out? Deals rely on relationships. Regardless of the industry you're in, you need the leverage of others to pull you through.

TACTICAL TAKEAWAYS

- Follow the Yellow Brick Road. Follow the money or better yet, let it follow you.
- It is always better to have options when raising money and definitely better to have options when dealing with VCs. Always get one or more investors interested in your deal so you can maintain critical things like valuation and vision.
- Keep your eyes on the ball. Make sure your date (VC) really likes you and the deal. It's like a marriage, so choose your mate wisely.
- If you have the right partner in your VC and you have followed the steps along the Yellow Brick Road then you may just have a soul mate.

Insider's Viewpoint

Greg A. Ray, CEO of ISB Global and International Speakers Bureau, Serial Entrepreneur, and Author of Business Parables 2 *Scoops Please* **and** *Why Johnny Can't Lead*

I have been blessed over the years to work with the most influential and recognized business executives, personalities, and thought leaders around the world. Back in 1990s, when we built WYNCOM, our team was responsible for helping brand and grow the GURU genre that included authors like Tom Peters, Michael Hammer, and Stephen Covey. It was a front row seat on the entrepreneur express with many twists and turns, not the least of which was raising institutional capital among the elite private equity firms in the world, and then working in a major venture-backed company as a CFO and director. That ride stopped on the edge of going public in a first-tier IPO when the CEO decided to pull the plug and fire the management team—yes, me too—on the front page of the *Wall Street Journal*. The headline read "Thriving on Chaos." How do you like those apples?

This was one of many deals I have been involved with as an investor, operator, and a guy who likes to step up to the plate. I, of course, can't for a moment leave my friend Billy G out here—his team and funds have invested almost $20 million in the various ventures I have been involved with. From the good, bad, and ugly sides, I have seen every angle of a deal, term sheet, venture capitalist mindset, and entrepreneur's

(Continued)

dilemma. It is quite a ride building a business, raising money, and even more so working between the investors and the entrepreneurs—it is often a very uncomfortable position to be in. This chapter hit it all on the head—it really is dating and marriage and the ups and downs of expectations and commitments without time to adequately look ahead or adjust the rear view mirror.

I have seen deals blow up over ridiculous and trite personality differences, greed, and just outright primal behavior. I have seen deal success led by powerful personalities with an all-out drive to succeed, with all stakeholders in-line and pulling in the same direction. I have seen sideways deals, upside-down and right-sized; repeatedly in every case, across every deal, integrity, perseverance, a commitment to win, and an outright insane sense of urgency have been among the greatest traits I have recognized in those who win in the end. As CEO of the ISB Global and International Speakers Bureau, I can say that we are firmly staked in promoting the global conversation on leadership and organizational advancement, including bringing top-shelf authors and leading personalities to life for millions worldwide. We practice what we preach. We practice what Billy G preaches, too. Today, I am convinced more so than ever that, aside all the management and leadership techniques and rhetoric out there, the fundamentals of true leadership in business are always inherent in our interactions with others and how we treat them. Ultimately, it defines how people treat us in good times and bad. Integrity and honor when working together with anybody is paramount. It is the essence of being able to look your investors, clients, partners, employees, and board in the eye and no matter the news, good or bad, maintain their support and belief in you. "Business is war," as Billy G says. You do not want to be in a business foxhole with a bunch of cowards who will shoot you in the back as you run out to engage the enemy or competition. Pick your battles and your partners carefully. The best professionals, VCs, lawyers, dealmakers, and of course Billy G, have all showed me that when the war is raging, and the drums of success or failure are beating loudly, the best investors and the greatest entrepreneurs all stand up for what is right, and find a way to support the cause, no matter the circumstances.

I love this chapter and there are many lessons to be learned from it. Having lived many, most, well, frankly, all of them out loud, I encourage you to zone in. You don't want to miss a thing here, lose your head, or worse, risk being left behind.

THE TWO-BY-FOUR

8

A key component of survival is to understand what threatens it. Once you can identify and embrace that reality, you are well equipped to fight. Without that understanding, forget about it. Turn around right now and be prepared to be struck by a two-by-four because eventually it's bound to happen. Believe me—you just don't want it happening to you! Think *reality* and not what you think or want reality to be and certainly not what reality was. This isn't the time to relive your high school touchdowns. Forget about what great shape you used to be in, because whatever you imagine reality to be is most likely not today's reality. The best leaders and big winners out there focus sharply on today and what they can do right now to win tomorrow. The best only live by the truth and manage only with facts while using great vision to plan for the future.

Great companies assess danger in the competitive marketplace. They know their enemy and see traps before they are sprung. Their leaders understand a secret others don't—that it's better to change when your strengths are fully leveraged than be wounded by a competitor or forced to change when market conditions mandate. Jack Welch is a business genius and while commanding General Electric he created an internal commando team that consistently attacked their products, markets, and advantages to find holes and weaknesses. Better to find your own flaws and weaknesses than let a competitor do so!

As a venture capitalist interested in leadership ideals and philosophies, it's been my experience that those who comprehend the dangers and ways to thwart them, while embracing risk and change will create the biggest businesses and world-altering paradigms. The leaders who are living large on their current successes are the most vulnerable of all because often their success has blinded them.

Most people have heard of Manolete, the greatest and wealthiest bullfighter in the world. Manolete was a rock star in Madrid, renowned for his unique style, the admiration of beautiful women, and the respect of millions of fans. He was most intriguing for his confidence, charisma, and unique method of fighting the bull, and in the ring, Manolete was different. His trademark style during a fight was that he did not pull away with the cape as most bullfighters did, jumping backward when the bull passed to avoid being gored. Instead, Manolete stood his ground fearlessly, defeating more bulls and becoming more famous than any other bullfighter on earth. This legacy continued for years, until the day he let his guard down. Manolete had announced his retirement, but a young competitor emerged and challenged him to one final match. Manolete decided to do it, and during the fight he struck the bull in the side, and the crowd roared! Once again it seemed the great and unbeatable Manolete had been victorious. He turned his back to acknowledge the wild applause from the crowd. In the past the fight would be over, and the bull would die. But this one didn't. This bull was different. The wounded bull charged Manolete from behind, and gored him. Later that day, the great Manolete died, and the world was stunned.

MORAL OF THE STORY: DON'T GET WOUNDED

I've witnessed firsthand companies that get gored because they are ill prepared to deal with changing market conditions. Their leaders forget that sometimes change is like a tornado that blindsides the trailer park as opposed to a slow moving hurricane tracked by meteorologists every half hour on the major networks. Sometimes you wake up and the entire world has changed. The wife has left you, there's a note on the counter, and the pickup is gone. The world is different and Grandpa uses Google instead of the *Encyclopedia Britannica*.

Where do you stand in your business? Are you building something? Are you open to change? Or are you already riding so high on your success that you are bound to forget how fast things can shift? One thing for certain is that your competitor isn't just sitting around waiting for business to come his way. He's plotting and planning and by the time he attacks you may not even know what hit you.

Business competitors will often be like a two-by-four in that they have the ability to wreak violence on you or your business. Such savage business associates may come after your job or a promotion that was intended for you. Companies that were unknown to you may soon be sprouting up around you, positioned to turn your business into a dinosaur through their own advancements. Look at the onslaught of Google to Yahoo! and AOL, which are now both under siege. A business competitor can quickly devastate your own successes in a way you never saw coming.

I had an intimate and firsthand experience with PC Travel that was delivering a huge two-by-four to the travel agent industry, setting out to change the rules overnight. When companies began to offer individuals and large corporations the ability to buy air travel over the Web, the entire space and business model changed. PC Travel was a pioneer with a great entrepreneur at the helm. Whoops! Travelocity delivered a two-by-four through strong marketing, and no one ever knew who PC Travel was. The leaders of PC Travel had an innovative idea, but they didn't have the commitment to go full on and understand the danger in the marketplace. They underestimated the competition, refused to move headquarters to California, and made a series of other small but disastrous decisions. By the time they looked up from their hole in the wall in Raleigh, they were bankrupt—and Orbitz, Expedia, and Travelocity emerged victorious with billions in the founders' pockets.

Business has always been competitive and fierce, but it has intensified in recent years. You can't just buy a competitor anymore. That strategy isn't enough. In the new market, there aren't any hard and steadfast rules. Competition in the business world has progressed in a way similar to that of gang fighting. Gangs used to battle with their fists and live to see another day even if it was to fight again. Today, adolescents wield Uzis and handguns, and often-innocent bystanders will reap the collateral damage. Likewise, businesses have grown more and more cutthroat when it comes to encroaching on customers and clients. In the contemporary business world, only those who are entrepreneurial and think ahead will survive.

A two-by-four in the hands of the wrong person is analogous to certain types of business competitors; if you are not prepared, such competitors can be fierce and may have the resources to knock you and your business down.

If a two-by-four is used to hit someone over the head, it can be a deathblow. Such an attack, proverbial or physical, means the victim may not live to see another day. Being edged out in today's business world is likely to mean suffering a mortal wound. The velocity of business and innovation has grown at a rate 10 times that of the prior year, every year for the past decade. This means unparalleled access to information, a flattening world, and competitors around every corner waiting to take your office, your job, or your business. At least they haven't included husbands, wives, and offspring like in the days of the barbarians. But they are certainly likely to take food off your table.

When Andy Grove, co-founder of Intel, said, "Only the paranoid survive," he was certainly correct. If you are in the business world today and do not believe and operate out of this mind-set, you could be in for a rude awakening. It is quite easy to be passed up or knocked down and whether or not it has already happened to you, you are no doubt at risk for this possibility in the future. In no time, a top company can slip to number three or number nine.

THE GOOD NEWS

The silver lining is that it doesn't have to be that way. You do not have to get taken advantage of by the new kids in town, and you can and should protect yourself. Just as people get alarm systems to protect their families and homes from outside threats, you can protect your career and your business by taking action and not being complacent. In this regard, it is useful to examine businesses that are poised offensively, ready to weather the vagaries of a particular market sector.

Consider how Yahoo! and AOL.com might feel about Google. Like a snake in the grass waiting to pounce, Google popped up through its IPO and was standing with its head high above all the others competing for consumer attention. Looking back, it seems clear that it was easy to see coming, with the punch even telegraphed. Even so, no one expected it to be such a game changer, which it was, is, and will continue to be. If AOL.com does not spin out or go public (and soon) then where will it be? Perhaps become part of Google, or it may merge with Yahoo! to stave off Microsoft's Yahoo! acquisition attempts, or it may become part of MSN—who knows? It is clear everyone now wants to go toe to toe with Google—even Microsoft, the 800-pound gorilla. A company like AOL must be actively searching for ways to position itself to compete in the future. In addition to having a sophisticated early warning system, companies today should also be able to preempt their competition. Then, in the event of an attack from insiders looking to crush their business, they will be prepared.

THE STRATEGY

To best position yourself it is important to anticipate and defend against attacks from competitors. The ability to be flexible and prepared to retaliate will also be important. You will likely need to be able to retaliate with such massive force, strength, and will that no matter what attack comes at you, you can return the blow with equal force and remain standing. Survival requires that you adopt the mind-set of "act or be acted upon" and having some kind of corporate alarm system to identify potential threats is important. For large organizations, the best protection is likely to come from someone outside the business because such an individual will bring a fresh perspective and new ideas.

The two-by-four analogy is also illustrated through the first Gulf War. Leland Russell wrote a book called *Winning in Fast Time* with John Warden, a colonel famous for having developed the core of the battle plan against Iraq. Similar to the Napoleonic charge, the barbaric hordes, and the German blitzkrieg, warfare was forever altered through the implementation of his plan.

Colonel Warden's plan was a departure from more conventional strategies. The first part of the plan centered on systems thinking. The military was forced to rethink how its various branches were best used and decided upon a strategy comparable to an orchestra of war. Each unit, each branch, and each asset was a discrete platform. Each soldier, tank, ship, or plane—collectively, the entire armed forces—was a platform for delivering ordnance of all types, sizes, and specializations. Iraq was thus seen as an organism with inflection points such as eyes, ears, arms, legs, veins, a brain, a heart, and a spine. In virtually the first 14 minutes of the war, Iraq was completely and utterly defeated.

More than 400 inflection points were targeted by stealth fighters, tomahawk missiles, B-52s, ships, and artillery, and it all happened in the first 14 minutes. Given this orchestral assault, Iraq was unable to defend itself on any substantive level. A similar idea applies to our businesses. We need to know that each aspect of our business contributes to the whole. We need to ensure that each department, division, employee, and leader is primed to help win the war in the business community. You must also determine key inflection points in your business and know how to press them to drive innovation, transformation, and, if necessary, complete revolution.

Extreme action or intervention will sometimes be necessary because many people require a radical departure from the regular way of doing business. In a world that is quickly and constantly changing, even the best of us can get run over if we are not prepared and on guard. Is it time to change your way of managing or thinking? If you're a leader, it might be time to switch up the team. It may ultimately bring you comfort and add great strength to your business when you have at your side a commando, a bodyguard, and at least one person who is paranoid all the time.

Everyone has a competitor. If you work for a major corporation you have one, (either inside or outside the organization), and if you're an independent business owner or entrepreneur you have one. Understanding your competitor is essential to avoid being gored.

I've been on the inside of deals like Excite, Priceline, and dozens of other unusual ventures, and I've seen the carnage and the battles won or lost in a second. I helped acquire and commercialize iChat and the team was directed to sell it to major portals to gain enterprise software revenue. Whoops! This time I was the idiot—I guess we all were at the company. We never suspected it would become a phenomenon as a result of the Web companies pushing it out to their users. But it did. If I had a penny for every thought tapped out on SMS and instant messaging. . . .

Leaders who are unable to assess danger, and who get too full of themselves won't see the two-by-four coming. On the other hand, most maverick thinkers have a two-by-four ready and aren't afraid to use it.

Look at the future happening right now in the financial sector where LBO groups are going public and the new robber barons are inheriting massive contracts and sucking up all the war dollars right back into their coffers. The leveraged buyout industry has become huge! It's becoming the new financial business of the future just like the investment banks were in the 1990s. Truth is, sometimes the two-by-four can decimate industries, create change for the common good, and make a boatload of money for the mavericks. Some of the best companies in the world have been built by change agents. People who thrive on change, catalyze it, and seek it.

The theory of Left on Red is about change, which often means not following the rules. When the herd is traveling right, you go left.

Sometimes law and order must be disrupted to achieve a true breakthrough.

TACTICAL TAKEAWAYS

- Do whatever it takes to prepare your business for contingency. Prepare your systems, prepare personally, and prepare your business for radical innovations that can disrupt or dismantle your models.
- Test and retest response systems. Have strike teams go after key points of inflection in your business. Seek weakness from the inside out and outside in. Prepare, prepare, prepare—and not just for sales growth and acquisitions.

- A two-by-four in the hands of the wrong person is analogous to certain types of business competitors; if you are not prepared, such competitors can be fierce and may have the resources to knock you and your business down.

Insider's Viewpoint

Leland Russell, Award Winning Author of *Winning in Fast Time*

A two-by-four is a very interesting analogy in business today and certainly something I learned about when I was writing *Winning in Fast Time* with Colonel Warden the architect of the first Gulf War. The analogy is so fitting for many companies that are simply trapped in the old ways of doing things. The world is changing so fast that leaders are not able to keep up. They can't change on a dime and find the inflection points within their organizations to prepare for battle with often much faster and more aggressive companies. They walk into a fight with an olive branch and the other guy is carrying a two-by-four. You know the rest.

I have been leading organizations and worldwide efforts like the EastWest Institute using principles I have learned not only from very well run organizations but one of the best run organizations, the military. The action plans and impact we are able to serve up to companies has dramatic effects on productivity, innovation, leadership, and global collaborations. It is simply amazing what can happen when a company faces issues head on and drives a stake right into the heart of the matter.

I have always believed that organizations must do three things in order to implement any plan, lead in an industry, and to compete effectively:

1. Think strategically
2. Focus sharply
3. Act swiftly

The principles sound simple but when dealing with giants like Texas Instruments and Weyerhaeuser it takes an all-out effort on a massive scale with global collaboration to win and avoid allowing another competitor to hit you in the head with a death blow.

At Geo Group we have dealt with the most serious issues that face mankind today. We have seen the results of nonaction, wrong action, and hesitation by companies and governments. Billy is right! Fear causes hesitation and hesitation causes your worst fear to come true. Today, in the global political and military climate and the business landscape speed is an awesome weapon as you read in the example of Iraq—speed and focus can utterly crush a competitor.

9

THE INTELLECTUAL DESERT

As has been true in the past and will likely be true far into our future, it is a fact that small segments of our society determine the fate of most everyone and everything pertaining to our species.

I point this out because most everyone falls into the "watching it happen" category. They are programmed by magazines, television, the workplace, the rat race, and other influences. Most are watching a life someone else designed and there is no control of destiny, no control of aspiration, and little or no control of self. It is not until you first realize the trap and see it for what it is that you can rise above the fray.

One percent of society manages and owns everything that the remaining part of society consumes. But this can go on only so long, until the new generations rise and take their positions in leadership. Once they do, everyone else will gain from it. Consider, for example, Alfred Nobel and his great vision for the Nobel Prize that created a lasting legacy for generations to come. However, simple math will tell you that the population at the top of the world's oligarchy doesn't change. It gets smaller and smaller and power is further and further consolidated and the rules bestowed upon us are there to thwart all but the lucky few from ever joining their ranks.

Society itself is an intellectual desert! Buy more stuff, take mindless trips to the mall, surf the Net and buy even more stuff we all don't need. Consume! Consume! Consume! Buy what we sell you, eat what we give you, look the way we say, and always have the carrot of the American Dream—glory and power—dangling on TV, in magazines, radio, music, Hollywood, and every medium of expression there is. Most of us have forgotten to stop, take a breath, and step off the roller coaster and out of the rat race and look at it for what it is. Hijacking! Theft of your free will and thought, your mind, body, spirit, creativity, and your wallet. Most everyone just goes along.

Be very aware that the world we now exist in is an intensely media driven world, and you have probably been hijacked right into it.

THE ART OF DISCOVERY

Look up tonight or on any clear night for a minute and imagine. The billions of stars you see in the night sky represent our galaxy, our neighborhood in space. The Milky Way is some 100 light years across. A light year equals 5.88 trillion miles. Put 100 times that into your calculator. We are significant insignificance—a tiny blue speck in a remote spiral on one galaxy too large to imagine.

But check this out: As vast as our galaxy is and as incomprehensible the trillions of miles between each star, it is just one of hundreds of millions and perhaps billions of galaxies that we have discovered with the help of the

Hubble telescope. You need a supercomputer to calculate that. What do you really have to lose in light of your position in time and space, among all those stars and galaxies? Pride? Money? A job? Seriously—take one step back and full stop! Asses it all—this isn't a fire drill. You have to get into the right mindset to loosen up and allow some thoughts to flow. In order to take scary and risky steps you have to realize there is nothing to lose after all.

It is very simple to understand. When you feel trapped in your mind or the world around you, constrained by the rules created by others who make you play their games, remember you are but a speck in the sands of time, a part of something unimaginably vast and certainly much greater than what you are stuck in. In other words, go for it! Vow to make a difference! Put your foot down and force yourself to take chances—create your own games and rules, try hard and fail sometimes, in fact fail many times if you have to. The only way to achieve success will be to just reach out, take the plunge, and go for it. Your success is your responsibility; it's the end of all things for you. Don't you want your life to count for something? You need some time to cast the disorder and mental captivity aside—if even for a little while—so you can let your imagination free up some computing power. In order to create something new and exciting you have to first imagine it!

Remember when you were a kid? You could follow a butterfly in flight through an empty field for a mile chase a can down a stream without concern. You could build a fort in the woods, ride bikes and shoot cap guns, play kick the can or hide-and-seek. Your imagination was strong, flourishing and overflowing with hope, joy, and a future full of opportunity. And then one day, you woke up. Do you remember when you first woke up?

Most people can't pinpoint the moment they lost the ability to dream. Visionaries think like a child, seeing life through the lens of *anything is possible*. I see creative minds with ideas in incubation all the time, and it inspires.

Everyone has heard the stories about techno geeks in jeans riding their Vespas to work, and the employees at dream houses like Ideo in Illinois who have bikes propped up against the wall in the lower level and crazy things hanging from their ceiling over a wide open, dreamy space designed to foster free thinking. You may not be in that type of environment now, but you can create it from within. You once had it, and you can get it back. It's time to think about creating new games and rules for yourself and others to play by.

Taking back time is your responsibility and yours alone. The only thing that has to change is your perception. Perception is the major driver of all change that takes place in your life. Once your eyes are open to new possibilities, you will never go back to your old way of thinking. You'll be like George Jefferson—once you move on up to the East Side, you ain't going back. Your perception has changed and you will fight for it every day with vigor.

WAKE UP AND SMELL THE COFFEE

After my own awakening, I headed from New York City to greener pastures in North Carolina's Research Triangle Park—home to various technology endeavors such as Cisco, Nortel, Lucent, Red Back, and IBM. It was the home of Internet II and an underexploited, underrecognized, underdeveloped center of gravity.

Upon arrival, broke but full of life and dreams, I stripped my clothes off and I scrubbed my body clean of the stench of corporate America. I decided I would never adhere to other people's opinions or rules, likes or dislikes, and I became the game. The game maker! I was no longer a piece on the chessboard of life. I was determined to build my own machine and create new rules of engagement. Talk about a feeling of freedom!

It may not be for everyone, but starting out on my own was the first step toward becoming who I authentically felt I needed to be and the life I wanted to live.

TACTICAL TAKEAWAYS

- The intellectual desert is vast. Most do not realize that they are trapped in it.
- The best way to avoid the desert is to be self-reliant and resilient and to use every minute you have to improve yourself so you are always an asset to the business you are in and a sought after asset with skills beyond the four walls.
- Perception is one thing we can change that will have major implications in our lives.
- Be a game maker not a player, and whatever you do, don't wind up a pawn on the chessboard. Your likelihood of success on any level will be greatly enhanced if you are in control of your destiny and making your own rules.

Insider's Viewpoint

Eric Becker
Founder, Sterling Ventures

I have the unusual pleasure of having to write about the intellectual desert, the terrain my family and our

(Continued)

companies are all focused on traversing. We recently took the companies my family built—Sylvan Learning and Laureate—from public to private, a reversal of sorts. It is poetic.

Our focus has been in education and educational improvements.

Teach them how to fish and they will never go hungry. We have truly led blessed lives and have passed on many blessings to society in the hope that we may provide a way for others to achieve and navigate the intellectual desert.

RETURN ON INNOVATION

Return on investment (ROI), the traditional measure for calculating economic returns just doesn't cut it anymore. Traditional ROI can't contemplate the true drivers of innovation. The old model of money in, money out, even risk-adjusted, isn't enough to get you there. Today's model for ROI is return on innovation, where innovation represents a force multiplier exponentially increasing the basic return on investment.

The velocity by which innovation is conducted creates a multiplier effect dependent on how intelligently an individual, group, or business can access critical relationships.

$ROI^{Innovation}$

The investment made in a company, business plan, product, or technology is heavily dependent on how innovative it is. Innovation can be broken down into chunks and accelerated and influenced by several variables. These variables will dictate an exponent that will actually drive the return on investment, which we call return on innovation.

Innovation has been redefined. There are five core areas that are critical to successful innovation that smart businesses and leaders are embracing. Each one of them affects you, and how well you and your business will thrive or merely survive. Companies and people who understand and develop these five cornerstones and effectively implement them, in parallel and with speed, will become true innovators. They will be able to explode growth in the most turbulent of market conditions and have a better than average shot at pulling away from the pack—as long as the idea itself has merit, of course, and is not the next kitty litter disposal unit.

From a venture capitalist's ivory tower, the core five areas of innovation are:

1. Ideation
2. Presentation
3. Deployment
4. Perseverance
5. Collective IQ

These areas are all influenced by the most critical factor—velocity!

BREAKING DOWN THE ELEMENTS OF INNOVATION

The first, ideation, is simply intelligently identifying ideas that have a "system fit" and providing the focus needed to direct organizational and/or personal resources toward their accomplishment. This requires the ability to recognize new paradigms and consider the full implications they represent.

The second element is presentation. Successful leaders understand the critical nature of their presentations and develop the ability to clearly articulate their vision, clearly define their plan for strategic action, and rapidly gain critical support for their innovative initiatives, inside and outside the organization. They can educate and make investors, customers, employees, and influencers understand their vision and how they will make it a reality.

The third factor is deployment, in which the effective organization is structured, focused, and equipped to effectively execute new business practices and frame the correct elements (money, management, operations, marketing, public relations, capital, and so on) around the idea.

The fourth is perseverance; innovative cultures are wired for resilience and able to endure the associated difficulties and predictable setbacks of breaking new ground.

The fifth element is collective IQ. Left on Red companies build the networks necessary to develop critical centers of gravity that provide access to partnerships, leaders, and influencers. They can leverage any and all influence they may require to get the job done on any scale. (And they build these networks before they need them.)

How well does your organization compete in these areas? These are the five areas of the future, and everything hinges on them.

Velocity is the most important factor of all. At one time I had a big sign on my wall that said: Speed Kills. Get Out of My Way!

How fast can you get things done? The speed at which people think, feel, and do today is mission critical. Speed has become a weapon of choice for many, and if others are using this armament and you are not, be assured that they will beat you to the punch every time.

Number 1: Ideation

The ability to see the unfolding patterns of the future and recognize the emergence of new paradigms or governing rules that suggest fresh ways to interpret our surroundings. This is ideation, and it's not to be taken lightly. As we've all seen with Google, a new paradigm can create a new business ecosystem. When this shift occurs, the new ecosystem eliminates old ways of doing business and gives rise to innovative opportunities. This is ideation at its finest.

Innovation leaders understand each idea coherently in the context of the new paradigm. To create value, each new creation must have a place, a fit into the new paradigm. Failure to understand innovative ideas in the context of the new business model increases the likelihood that the innovation will die for lack of support within the new business ecosystem. Like Nobel, who formed the paste into dynamite, naming the ingredients as well, new ideas must fit into the economy rapidly to create value, because ideas that don't or no longer fit are dispatched equally quickly. You build it and they will come only works some of the time. Ideas have to be able to fill a need or a gap or expand upon an existing way of doing things.

Number 2: Presentation

Visionary leaders look at the business landscape and see the future, while most people look at the same set of conditions and only see the present. Innovation leaders see what's possible and needed before others are capable of seeing it or are ready to understand it. Because the window of opportunity to take innovation from idea to action is breathtakingly short, innovation leaders must be able to rapidly get others on board—this includes all stakeholders who are affected by or who can affect the success of the innovation.

The innovator's view is of the unfamiliar—which represents change. How do you present a view of the future that only you can envision? Presentations are the tool that innovation leaders use to influence others and enlist critical support. Any veteran of the venture industry knows how critical one presentation can be to the success or failure of an idea, an individual, or a leader. Venture capitalists see it every day.

Number 3: Deployment

Assume for a second that your innovative idea establishes a marketplace footing. Now the real fun begins! People and operating parts of the business must be tuned up and strategically deployed in such a way that results and expectations are coherent and crystal clear. Sharp deployment means having real-time dashboard indicators and good field intelligence. All working parts must be continuously monitored for performance and results and running on all cylinders.

Number 4: Perseverance

Early American pioneers got hurt and took arrows. Trailblazing ain't for the weak of heart. Maintaining mental toughness is required for staying the course long enough to make breakthroughs. The innovation process by definition means going into unfamiliar territory. The difficulty of implementing innovation requires emotional and psychological endurance. In a time when people are increasingly being asked to do more with less or risk being outsourced overseas, innovation can be seen as another straw threatening to break the camel's back. Innovation leaders develop mental toughness in both themselves and those in their organizations.

This message is critical: You will fail! Fail with pride. Be happy and proud of your failures. Consider them battle stripes on your sleeve. It may even mean that at some point you'll experience heavy debt, a leveraged house, or the borrowing of family and friends' money, (though I'm not endorsing any of it!), which, for an entrepreneur, can be considered par for the course. Most people simply cannot stomach the weight of this.

Number 5: Collective IQ (Intelligent Access)

The shelf life of a great idea can be measured in nanoseconds. Even with the support of a good management team and financial backing, most innovative ideas are threatened at conception by competing ideas in the marketplace. It is Darwinism in an instant: Darw-instantism. Like a thoroughbred getting out of the gate, if an idea doesn't get instant traction it's out of the race for good.

To get a good footing means instantly having traction and securing centers of gravity in the areas of the business ecosystem critical for success. The emergence of an idea in the marketplace must take place instantly and it must be substantial enough that the competitors in the market are outnumbered or outgunned.

The capable visionary leader knows this and has a deep network of allies that can be called upon. These allies give the idea a footing. Unfortunately, during a paradigm shift many of the allies and footings are no longer obvious, and it takes more than just a deep Rolodex, it takes an intelligent Rolodex—one that identifies and provides access. This collective IQ is the ability to see the necessary supporters within new business ecosystems and access them in a compelling way. This new form of social capital extends beyond simple access to knowledge and contacts. It is intellectual property combined with horsepower, momentum, and execution. It's the ability to make things happen and often to move mountains.

Velocity

$V = D/T$.

We all learned that one in physics. Well, in today's world a new periodic table of business elements has emerged from my hands to yours and the alchemy of putting them together begins here. Business Velocity = $(I + A + E)$

This is your IQ (Intellect) + Access (Your Collective IQ above) and Execution.

How smart are you?

Let's assume for a minute that you are a pro ball player and you get on the court with a high school all-star. Absolutely, after the first dunk the lesser competitor knows in his heart he is outmatched. You get it don't you? High IQ on the court means you get it—and I mean fast—and you're a cut above and a faster, more cognitive thinker than those around you. You can race in 12 directions and get from A to Z before the second sentence is out of their mouths.

Next is access and intelligent access at that. This is what we call collective IQ. Collective IQ is the name my partner Jon Nieman and I gave our company, which we formed around a vast network of intellectuals—business, social, economic, and scientific leaders around the world. This is our Skull and Bones, the result of more than 20 years of helping friends and colleagues into positions of influence all over the world in music, film, technology, venture capital, publishing, radio, TV, investment banking—you name it.

Real power comes when you can leverage your intellect, and more importantly others', to access the right people at levels high enough to move a mountain. In doing so you can follow through on what people say they need—as well as your instinct and intuition on what they couldn't even envision they need. If you pull it all together and deliver it wrapped in a pretty bow—BOOM—you'll break the business sound barrier and leave quite a few people with their jaws open.

LEFT ON RED ORGANIZATIONS

The breakthrough companies that affect world and social transformation are like Nobel, actively seeking people who think differently. They are Apple, Google, Cisco, Upromise, and Nokia, and they don't follow traditional rules. Like Nobel, who himself had been homeschooled, sheltered from the traditional rows of desks, order and processes, these organizations have no boundaries that limit them. It makes no difference what's being done. It makes no difference what is real and probable. The only thing that matters is what can be.

Early on in life, Nobel developed a penchant for chemistry. Those around him encouraged his curiosity and he began experimenting with a way to manufacture nitroglycerine using a detonator and black gunpowder. After several failures and successes in adulthood, Nobel and his associates realized that nitroglycerine had to be absorbed by some kind of porous material. He found it in the sand in Germany, of all places, and was able to form a paste that was easy to knead and shape. It was molded into rods that were easily inserted into drilling holes, and he named it "dynamite" from the Greek word *dynamis*, meaning power.

Dynamite changed the way the world was and still is built. Why didn't anyone else think of it? In venture capitalist circles I see this all the time. Someone thinks of an idea, presents it, but doesn't have the guts, brains, street smarts, perseverance, proper ideation, or collective IQ to make it happen. And then sometimes along comes a person with all of those things, and more. Where are you?

TACTICAL TAKEAWAYS

- The success of an investment made in a company, business plan, product, or technology is heavily dependent on how innovative it is and the speed at which the idea can be capitalized, connected with critical relationships, and brought to market ahead of or with overwhelming force against a competitor product or service.
- Innovation is a force multiplier for companies and people alike. Innovation, an often overused word, can be broken into key elements that in concert can move an idea from incubation to reality to success.
- Left on Red companies build the networks to develop critical centers of gravity that provide access to partnerships, leaders, and influencers.

- Businesses, entrepreneurs, and intrapreneurs have to realize that velocity is the most important weapon in the innovation arsenal.
- You have to have an absolutely ridiculous sense of urgency. Only the most paranoid survive.

Insider's Viewpoint

Jon Nieman, Vice Chairman, Co-Founder, Collective IQ
Former Pension Advisor for More Than $150 Billion in Private Equity

I have been in investment banking and private equity for more than 30 years. I have played the game with household names and titans of industry. We always spoke frankly and everything we did had a specific bottom line or return on investment (ROI).

It is a simple concept. How much money did I invest and over time how much money did I get back in return? It's straightforward to calculate and always provides a measure by which the investment banking and private equity industry judges itself.

Then along comes somebody complicating things again. However, when you think about it the principles of return on innovation speak to drivers that have come of age. Exponential returns based on elements and drivers such as velocity are incredibly insightful and capture the essence of what financial markets have long understood but haven't had a road map to follow.

Having dealt with entrepreneurs of all makes and models and deal makers at the highest level, I recognize the implications of each principle defined as a component of innovation. The Rolodex, more than any other element, has the most dramatic influence on a company's ability to succeed and succeed fast. My advice is be connected or get connected. Move faster than the other guy.

11

GO LARGE OR
GO HOME

Anyone who believes there's always tomorrow in today's fast-paced world is going to miss out on the opportunities of today. There is no tomorrow.

I've been known to ask people to listen to the following phrases and tell me which one is true.

Patience is a virtue.

The tortoise beats the hare.

There's always tomorrow.

If you are in technology or a venture-backed company and you answered "true" to any of these—then hurry up and bury your head in the sand for the next decade because in today's business environment there is no tomorrow and the tortoise gets smoked by the hare every time. The best innovators have funnel vision and are able to execute with *velocity* and use a powerful collective IQ to outpace and outstrip anyone's ability to even be on the same playing field. The stagnant are those who believe any one of those phrases is true.

Patience is rarely a virtue anymore, especially if you're presenting your business to a venture capitalist and have to beat others to market. The tortoise is slow, plain and simple, and generally, the fastest one wins the race. And anyone who believes there's always tomorrow is likely to miss out on the opportunities of today. Sometimes, tomorrow doesn't exist and if you still believe it does when it comes to business, you need more than a paradigm shift to survive the future! Your thought processes have to change plain and simple, in order to gain the edge needed to stay ahead of the pack.

"Go large or go home" is a simple phrase I borrowed from friends at Excite @Home. It's self-explanatory and a rule to live by in today's business culture. If you are not out to win, to go global, and dominate your industry, niche, or category then stay in bed, call in sick, or simply run away. It may not be in California or Boston or Austin, but the competition is coming and it may come out of the woodwork from London, New Delhi, Beijing, Tokyo, Tel Aviv, or who knows where else.

The name of the game is sprint. That's right, run as fast as you can and don't look around to see what the other guy is doing because if he's smart he's running as fast or faster than you are. That's the nature of the beast. Prudence and thoughtfulness have their place, but hurry up already, make decisions, be decisive and aggressive, and get up to the plate and knock one out of the park. You can still have a vision of the big picture and execute, but a mere survival strategy just won't cut it any longer. Let's use an example.

Compare Amazon.com's market capitalization in September 1999 to other retailers in its space. You could add JCPenney and Kmart to the comparison and it would make the point more clear. Do you think that Barnes & Noble or Borders woke up one day and saw Amazon.com coming? Nope. BAM! They were hit by a proverbial two-by-four before they even knew what hit them. Amazon could engulf the whole retail supply chain and you'd soon be visiting the Amazon.com bookstore in your local mall. For all the MBA students reading this, do me a favor and run this one through your Black-Scholes model. You won't find much.

The new business model is *Revolution not Evolution*. What do you think the Romans thought about the Visigoths or Marie Antoinette about the peasants in France? What will you think when that 19-year-old on a PC in Singapore beats you like a drum and whittles away at your customer base? It's likely that you won't believe patience is a virtue, and you won't believe there is a tomorrow anymore.

Let's take a peek at a visual of Evolution versus Revolution.

Evolution Compared to Revolution—March 1999

Volvo	Geo Cities
▪ 72-Year-Old Automaker	▪ 2 Years Old, $0 Revenue
▪ Sold to Ford—Appx $5 Billion	▪ Sold to Yahoo!—Appx $5 Billion
▪ Ford—Founded 1908	▪ Yahoo!—IPO 1996
▪ $20 Billion Revenue	▪ $200 Million Revenue
▪ MKT Cap $61 Billion	▪ MKT Cap $31.6 Billion

The Volvo model depicts a 72-year-old company sold for approximately the same amount as a 2-year-old company. Times have changed. Is it time for you to rethink the importance of historical data and start focusing on the things you can't yet see? The future, and being able to predict it, is the single most important indicator of success.

If you're going to look back, look at the battle strategies of great warriors and apply them to your current business strategy. Go big or go home. I'm not suggesting lawlessness or ruthlessness, but Attila the Hun is a great example of how to take no prisoners in business. When the barbaric horde he commanded set forth to take over a land, hundreds of thousands of warriors, miles wide, would drive every living animal including humans into the middle of a large circle. Then for days, weeks, months, however long it took, every living thing was slaughtered. The killing went on until his youngest son would ask for the life of one creature to be spared. Are you kidding? What an intimidating tactic. Go large, be intimidating, and make others run away before they're even a threat. If you have to compete and battle it out, well, you better take control of that sandbox and take their milk money if necessary. If they aren't crying and whining inside their heads and inside their business—then they may be able to get up and fight another day!

One thing is absolute and history proved it to be certain. The ruthless tactics caused fear and trepidation and all-out capitulation in the next land to be conquered. Attila rode forward without raising a sword. Word had spread and fast. Who would want to face that enemy? It was the same with Alexander the Great. Nations would lay down their arms rather than fight the monster.

Business is war. Ancient warriors never backed down. Look around and you'll find that today, the best businesses still draw from ancient strategists in their determination and commitment to dominate. I won't even quote Sun Tzu here and tell you what you have probably heard a hundred times already.

Take a look at Netscape again, with its huge IPO in the early 1990s that set off the Internet gold rush and the age of the new robber barons. Netscape was huge. It was an 800-pound silverback gorilla beating its chest, until along came King Kong. Microsoft was better positioned, better armed, and just outright more ruthless. Microsoft, like Attila, had a take-no-prisoners strategy and absolutely decimated Netscape. By building Internet Explorer into Windows in one move, it decapitated, stomped on, and beat down Netscape. Microsoft understood that no matter what the price, the on ramp to the future was the Internet browser, and it had to own it. Scott McNeely, the brilliant founder of Sun Microsystems, lobbied the government along with other technology gang members to sue Microsoft for unfair business practices and antitrust violations. At the end of the day, it didn't work. They looked like crybabies and the spotlight on Microsoft simply highlighted its technical oligarchy.

Go large or go home. From then on history repeated itself, just like in the days of Attila. All Microsoft had to do was announce it was heading in a direction or point toward a market and the landscape became a tundra. It would just freeze. Competitors became deer in headlights while Microsoft picked apart business plan after business plan, and business after business, until the others simply laid down their arms and surrendered their revolutionary technology and category-leading positions to Uncle Bill.

FOOD FOR THOUGHT. WORDS TO THE WISE. AND HERE'S SOME ADVICE

For the entrepreneurs out there, sprint.

Find the best people. Be serious and get the best talent money can buy. If you have a small or medium-size business, you need great people to succeed. If you have a larger venture, you may be the one to take your own deal public or get it sold but don't be shy, because you may have a lot of equity riding on it. If your ego gets in the way of bringing in better management talent or better technical talent than yourself, it's going to be a problem.

Find great partners. The people and businesses you partner with can make or break you. Today, social capital is the key to growth because your collective intelligence can become a powerhouse that dominates. If you are taking a Left on Red and you've left the business without a net then make sure your venture capitalist—if you have one—and your angel investors are your partners. In my business, these partnerships are like matrimony. Just like a marriage, you are wed in the deal. Your goals and aspirations should be aligned. If you're going to find a VC make sure you find one that has connections—and big ones. Test his track record with his portfolio executives. Ask him to allow you to speak with others who have taken money from him, and don't be shy. In fact, turn right and cough.

Relationships are essential. If you think that you can go it alone in today's fast-paced world, or you want to hide your discovery and have everyone sign a nondisclosure statement to talk to you, great, see you on the other side. While you are tinkering around, your competitors are aligning themselves with every channel partner, strategic technology partner, and customer before you will ever have a chance. Identify potential strategic partners up front. Invite them in to help you develop and refine your business model or technologies. Give them equity in return for integration or early adoption. Do whatever it takes to get the industry pregnant with your product. And by the way, do it quickly because everyone else is.

MARKETING, MARKETING, MARKETING

"If we only get 1 percent of the market, we will be worth a billion." Really? I can't tell you how many times I've heard that. If you are after 1 percent of any market—go home! Think bigger. Win, win, win. Sound your trumpet and blow your horn—as loudly and often as possible. Get your name on a stick and push it up above the fray and all the noise in the industry, because if you don't someone else will. One of the biggest mistakes an emerging company can make is overlooking the importance of market visibility and awareness. I have seen many great technologies get crushed by companies with good marketing and inferior technology. Good marketing creates public perception. Public perception is a greater factor in creating value for companies today and in creating buying behaviors in customers than ever before. Perception is reality.

Speed

Getting to market faster than anyone else, getting your big ideas into the hands of consumers, and getting people to buy now, is key. We are in the era where information is transmitted around the world in seconds. Patience is not a virtue anymore.

Cash

Money makes the world go round. Worried about dilution? Think again. Money is the key to building a winning combination and a huge factor in accelerating and enhancing all of the previous activities mentioned. When you can get money, get a lot of it. Move past valuation, although it is important, look at the big picture. Money is a weapon and if you get hung up on maintaining control of your business and keeping a huge percentage for yourself, oftentimes you won't find the right partners with the right resources. Most major VCs will take a minimum of 25 percent of your company. Why? Because they can? No. They are heavily connected to all the resources just mentioned and can get you where you need to be very quickly if they are any good. They want to be successful, too, and they are entrepreneurs themselves. The quality of the money is more important than the quantity in most cases. Ideally, you want both quality and quantity, but money for the sake of money won't be any help in building your business quickly, and speed is the most critical factor today.

If you are in business or getting into business, your weapons are your talents, your people, your technology, your partners (technical and financial), your money, and most of all the ability of you and your partners to execute. Your competition is only a click away.

TACTICAL TAKEAWAYS

- Patience is rarely a virtue anymore, especially if you're presenting your business to a venture capitalist and have to beat others to market. The tortoise is slow, plain and simple, and generally the fastest one wins the race.
- Go large or go home. Anyone who believes there's always tomorrow is likely to miss out on the opportunities of today. Sometimes, tomorrow doesn't exist.
- Velocity and media are among the most powerful weapons of the twenty-first century. Make sure all the elements of the businesses are aligned – management, money, and operations. Use the media and move extremely fast to outpace your competitors.
- Cultivate the Left on Red maverick thinkers who can transform your business—or be one yourself.

Insider's Viewpoint

Matthew Growney, Founding General Partner, Rudyard Partners
Co-Founder and Former Managing Director, Motorola Ventures

I have invested in 40 technology businesses and have gotten my hands dirty building them. I have never taken to the notion of building a good company. I only wanted companies that would be great. I valued companies and management that understood what it meant to go after a new market and win, rolling over

(Continued)

or through whatever stood in the way of success. It took aggression, intelligence, and a lot of hard work, but we got many companies acquired and on their way to becoming public.

I have seen the best of deals and the worst of deals from both the inside and outside. No formula is a winner every time but companies that combine great management, adequate capitalization, large go-to-market partners, and an unbelievable sense of urgency often have an edge on their competitors. Obviously, the business must have real technology, a dominant product or service, and a major market opportunity, in other words, a solution that isn't a round peg trying to fit in a square hole.

My experience leads me to believe that innovative disruption in industries and even in companies comes from big thinkers with big ideas. It's rare for most people to even understand what entrepreneurs or intrapreneurs have their minds around and hands on. But if you have market intuition and can gauge the market's future with an understanding of the core offering, it'll make for a great marriage between the venture capitalist and your entrepreneurial team. (That is, assuming of course, you aren't going after 1 percent of some market and lack the stomach to dominate an industry.)

IV

The Strength of
Social Capital

SHAKING HANDS AND KISSING BABIES

In the heyday of the technology boom I sat on the board of a magazine called *Upside*, the first technology publication about people, personalities, and deal making. This is where Tony Perkins, the founder of *Red Herring*, and Eric Knee of *Forbes ASAP*, emerged from. *Upside* was the first to build technology events and to promote technogeeks and VCs as rock stars. In the past, technology companies were just technology companies, like any other company in another industry. But *Upside* shined a spotlight on hot new technology employees and technogeeks, like *Rolling Stone* magazine promotes bands and rock stars, or *Sports Illustrated* promotes top athletes! It was a big thing to be featured in *Upside*. I learned through that experience the value of social capital and networks. The people you surround yourself with can transform your life and your business.

BUILDING YOUR COLLECTIVE IQ

In the early days of building my business I worked hard and sought out people who had big Rolodexes and major influence. I came across soon-to-be partner Jay Allen who built the CXO Network in Colorado that has spread to many states and represents one of the best-organized networks in the country. Like LinkedIn, we had developed a massive but proprietary Rolodex feeding and building upon itself, and we always kept in mind the principles of providing free access to our ideas.

Many carefully nurture their Rolodexes and networks and make a lot of money doing it. My biggest mentor and friend Joel Katz showed me how to value myself and my network and turn it into gold. The network multiplication effect is profound and transforming. Joel was ranked by *Forbes* as one of the 10 most powerful deal-making attorneys in the country. For years, I've worked in the music industry beside this media icon, and he has often connected me with people I needed to know to help get something done. I've learned a lot just through observation.

Shaking hands and kissing babies is exactly what an extrovert networker does from a stage, a TV show, or in person. I used to have baby dolls in diapers all over my office, in chairs, and on cabinets. I like to keep things light in business and in politics so whenever a politician came by the office, I always had a baby ready—gotta make 'em feel comfortable! And that's all part of my authentic persona. Whether they like me or not, people remember me. I'm light and laid back and quick to find a solution or connect people.

How do you meet people and leave such an impression on them that they are never going to forget you? Think about your own networking IQ and what it is you can do to enhance it. When you meet someone the next time, or need to reach out to them, will they remember you? It's essential to have a network and be disciplined in the service of others without expecting anything in return. It will come back to you multiplied.

SUPERCONNECTORS—THE BLACK BOX

Clearly, as with everything else in the enterprise, the boss—the CEO—is ultimately in charge of ensuring that the organization's collective IQ is well above room temperature and sufficient to support innovation needs and goals. The CEO carries the message to key executives and staff who must understand and value the organization's collective IQ and actively support and nurture its growth and development.

However, the CEO in fact may not be the principal superconnector who staffs the nodes and minds the links on behalf of the top of the house. Why? CEOs have a full plate and maximizing collective IQ is real work and a full-time job in larger organizations. Moreover, the attributes, skills, and capabilities of a highly effective superconnector probably differ from the job requirements profile of many CEOs in several respects. Accordingly, while superconnectors must be close to the leader, they also must have the time, energy, and license to pursue their work without undue distraction. If you read *Tipping Point* this would go beyond the connector who can recall many names and dates and events. The superconnector has a rather large brain and can take disparate businesses and ideas and connect people in ways never thought of and create huge deals as a result. It's not just the network that moves mountains, it takes a talented mind to use it, to see the possibilities and make the impossible happen.

What Does It Take to Be a Great Superconnector?

For most businesses and professional organizations, we're talking about the need to build and maintain networks that involve hundreds or thousands of contacts, and on a basis much more intimate than just a list of names and numbers in a contact management file. Having the nimbleness of a nine-ball juggler and the memory of an elephant are entry-level requirements. But the superconnector can't simply be a walking database with the personality of a supercomputer; sincerity, likeability, and pleasantness all count as does having the patience and affability to put up with some valuable folks who may be difficult to get along with.

It means working with these contacts in very creative ways and finding potential relationships that aren't obvious, while arranging contacts in environments where the possibilities can unfold without a hint of contrivance.

It means setting things up and setting people up with ideation already introduced, and coordinating introductions made with intelligence as to why they should be speaking at all. It also means not doing stupid things and having the sense to know when an easy-to-make potential connection might be best left open because there are too many downside risks. Superconnectors don't purposely invite the fox into the henhouse.

It means having the tenacity to be in the game for the long haul. It requires sticking with people who clearly have something to offer but may not have a willing audience at the moment. At the same time, just as the gardener prunes regularly and selects new plantings with an eye to diversity, the superconnector sometimes needs to help the network stay healthy by moving some connections to reserve status.

Pruning and prioritizing are valid network maintenance options, but burning bridges, even with horrible miscreants, is usually not a good idea. Time has a way of changing perspectives. One example is Frank Abagnale Jr., the notorious forger and con man profiled in the movie *Catch Me If You Can*. He was later brought into the FBI's Intelligence Network and has gone on to be a major player on the side of good through his work with both the agency and with financial institutions worldwide.

How Do Superconnectors Provide Value? How Do They Get "Paid"?

The contributions of a functioning superconnector are not that complicated but they can be overlooked, trivialized, or undervalued by observers who do not see the critical connection between this role and the pace of innovation. Superconnectors are the *catalysts who make things happen* in places and ways that aren't always or immediately evident.

Connectors are power multipliers. Instead of losing power by giving it away, they grow it, and superconnectors grow it at awesome rates. They make big differences in areas that count by growing employment, expanding gross domestic product, and positively impacting social issues, much of the time with a completely below the radar profile.

The result of superconnectors' work isn't immediate or obvious and they aren't likely to be on stage for the applause but just to produce ideas and connect the dots for the crowd. Why then, would they pursue this work? Well for one thing, while the results are not immediate or obvious to the outside world, the superconnectors know exactly what they have caused to happen, and know it well in advance of the public unveilings.

For another, the experience of the superconnector is much like that of the hunter. Most of the joy is in the hunt not in the ultimate bagging of the game. Superconnectors are clearly "journey" people. While desired destinations are clearly in focus, arrival simply means the beginning of the next leg.

Yet another source of "income" for these special individuals is simply the enjoyment they get from personal relationships. They legitimately *like* people and don't maintain elaborate reciprocal bookkeeping systems to track who owes whom a favor.

Finally, when recognition does come from those they have touched, it comes in waves. Again, it isn't always seen clearly from the outside, but there are some markers—lineups at conventions and cocktail parties is just one example. For many observers, the whole network is totally invisible to the outside world until the funeral when huge attendance signals the real importance of the dearly departed. One could say that public recognition this late is regrettable, but if the superconnector were around to comment, he or she would say something like "Of course, I knew exactly who was coming . . . "

Who is the superconnector on your leadership team?

THE CHESSBOARD

This is not a test but you should really focus on it. No matter what you do and where you go it is always better to be able to know people in places of influence than not. My network methodically propelled more than 1,500 executives into power over 20 years. (Actually more, but they all don't work out.) How is that for a chessboard? I stacked the deck, and used national mediums to build my Rolodex and became the hub—the superconnector.

I always keep my database full and fill it all the time. Four or five times a year I write personal messages on birthdays, Father's Day, Mother's Day, and sometimes just to say hi. I wouldn't if I didn't genuinely want to keep in touch with the great people I have come to know.

In addition, I use PR to bring ideas and various business concepts and accomplishments to the media but even more so to the network to keep it fresh and active. We make phone calls and have created events to have regular gatherings of great minds. Now that's pretty darn hard to do when the rest of your life is so complicated and you are writing a book about it, but all the same it is power. Power comes in two primary forms: money, which is transient, and connections, which can never be taken away unless you violate their trust. Never lie, never shake a hand and change a deal, and always do what you say you will do for others—even if it isn't successful or you come out on the wrong end. Follow through exactly. Follow through is 90 percent of building relationships.

I'll be honest. I took my company name—Collective—from *Star Trek*. The Borg. The biggest, baddest species ever invented by Hollywood. Their overarching superiority and the fact they were linked to each other by one brain and central processor—or superconnector—was a profound theory. It created an almost invincible force that no species could defend itself against. They would simply roll up on whole planets and ships in space and say, "Resistance is futile. You will be assimilated," and that was it. They worked day and night for the collective good and consciousness. Collective IQ is just that—many brains linked together to expand the power of any company, executive, politician, or head of state by thinking beyond their wildest dreams and delivering ideas and partnerships on demand. That's the kind of network that works.

TACTICAL TAKEAWAYS

- How do you meet people and leave such an impression on them that they are never going to forget you? Think about your own networking IQ and what it is you can do to enhance it. How can you get people connected and create good ideas for them, so you are viewed as not just a collector of business cards but a connector adding value?
- It is essential to have a network. If you are not extroverted, align with organizations that have structure or find an ally who is.
- Superconnectors are the hub and have many spokes into their networks and those of others. Like a

supercomputer in the middle of the networks, superconnectors provide value for disparate companies, products, and people on the fly and around the clock. Their value is immeasurable. Be one and seek them. They are the real secret sauce, and you definitely don't want a competitor having one.

Insider's Viewpoint

Ross Reck, Author
The X Factor, Win-Win Negotiator
Revved, Co-Author with Harry Paul (Best-Selling Author of *Fish*)

Bulletproof Business Relationships

At birth, a new idea is vulnerable. Existing conditions in the marketplace, including inherent competitors, established interdependencies, and current equilibriums regarding allocation and consumption of resources stack the deck against the success of new entrants. For this reason, it is incumbent upon the innovator to work diligently through the gestation period to establish needed relationships; suppliers, channel partners, customers, and so forth so the idea emerges with points of strength or centers of gravity that give it enough grounding and strength to withstand the economic and competitive forces that will challenge it. This requires the ability to build strong and lasting business relationships; ones that are favorable enough to each party so that both parties are willing to grow and change their relationship as emerging conditions may require.

(Continued)

Which Set of Business Results Would You Like to Achieve?

A	B
Ordinary Results	**Extraordinary Results**
Barely surviving in a highly competitive market	Dominating a highly competitive market
Customers who shop for the lowest price	Customers who enthusiastically pay premium prices
Suppliers who fill orders	Suppliers who show you how to reduce costs
Employees who resist change	Employees who suggest change
Having to cold call new customers	New customers who call you
Implementing the latest management fad	Getting your current management system to work
Tension between labor and management	A 15-year labor agreement with annual double-digit productivity gains
Putting your destiny in the hands of others	Controlling your own destiny

If you chose column "B," you've identified yourself as someone who prefers taking charge and making things happen rather than following the crowd. You no doubt expect to achieve far beyond what most people would consider acceptable or good. You are not interested in ordinary or mediocre results; you want extraordinary results and are willing to work exceptionally hard to accomplish them.

Hard work, however, does not guarantee extraordinary results. You also have to know how to build and maintain bulletproof relationships with the people who stand between you and success or failure. You have to turn these people into enduring allies and partners who are excited about helping you achieve extraordinary results.

PENGUINS AND POLAR BEARS

Flipping television channels one evening, watching five programs at once like any obsessive compulsive armchair driver, I settled on a fascinating program on The Discovery Channel, where a group of penguins huddled together, bracing for a storm. The penguins were squawking or quacking, whatever it is they do, and just before I flipped the channel again, the camera quickly panned over to a hill. At the top, three polar bears appeared, and rapidly approached the penguins linked together like an avian chain.

The squawking and quacking and carrying on like a bunch of penguins is similar to what people do in the workplace when trying to protect themselves from perceived predators. They complain and whine about successful people and fight new ideas. There is chattering, back-stabbing, and what I call "black PR," which is PR that you don't even know is happening to you unless you look and listen really closely. Black PR is negative conversation that occurs behind your back and spreads like wildfire. It's something you have to stop and reverse. I don't engage in it because it is a sign of weakness and when people within organizations do it, it's as ineffective as a bunch of penguins and their huddled masses. What kind of a defense is that? Huddle together and form a smorgasbord for the polar bears.

PENGUINS

Humans, like penguins, tend to band together and brace for the storm when threatened by change. But that strategy is counter to their very survival, and in the end the weight and speed of change crushes them. Why didn't the penguins scatter to escape? Why don't employees and management prepare themselves better for competition, predators, and change? Couldn't they even predict the next move and get ahead of the curve instead of sitting behind the eight ball? The vast majority of people are employees and fall into a routine with corporate blinders on, become a cog in the wheel, or are content to push pens and paper across their desks.

For most people life is enjoyable, work is "fine, honey," and the dog barks by their white picket fence. The apple pie tastes good and the Chevy runs great. The sun comes up each day. But one day it may not; perhaps that day is already upon you or you expect it might be looming over the hill. Maybe it happened before and like a corporate addict in recovery you never even knew what hit you.

The fact is that many are comfortable. Are you? Seriously, are you comfortable, and do things seem stable? Life is good, right? Don't fall into the trap. Keep one eye over your shoulder and in the back of your head. Step up the pace and keep it up. Enjoy life and be content, but don't become someone else's food on the table.

As a venture capitalist, I've witnessed management teams, employees, and entire economic regions banding together in the hope that things would never change. They held the reins and built a corporate or regional oligarchy, so they couldn't imagine that even a single person or a wave would hit them and break through their huddle and rock their boat. But the outcome is rarely in the favor of the "old boys" or the bluebloods anymore. The cliques inside corporations unwilling to test limits and live in a constant state of readiness and fluctuation will absolutely fall prey to competition, and management that allows it to happen will be prey to a board or internal aggressiveness. That's the way the world is and the way life has become, especially a life in business.

CHAOS

Our world is already turned upside down. Corporate buyouts are rampant. Jobs are getting outsourced. Consolidations and forced retirements are commonplace. Eat or be eaten. Kill or be killed. It is as simple as that. The global economic shift thus far has been a ripple, but a huge wave is coming. Don't be trapped, drowned, or washed away as so many others have been.

How do you prepare for inevitable waves of change and unyielding upheaval in markets and inside the corporate walls and even in your life? Here is lesson one. Change is dynamic, fluid, and always happening with or without your participation. When the penguins resist, the polar bears get well fed. Two. Change occurs, and no form of defense other than a good offense will save you or the corporate team. When a corporation faces an anxious market or stock prices and sales are down, or when management stands huddled in a corner sweating bullets over its competition and earnings reports—guess what? The boat is sinking and they will throw out some weight fast to stay afloat. You know why? Mostly because they have no idea what else to do. Sometimes, unfortunately they think chopping heads is the only way out. With the inevitable right sizing and the cream rising to the top, ask yourself: Are you the tasty cream or sour milk, meat or fat?

I witnessed the banding together phenomenon in an entire region of North Carolina. I set my sights on success in an otherwise closed environment. The old guard had a solid foothold and a plan for the community already in place and that wasn't about to change. I was young, and there were very few who took me seriously, but my goal was simple. In finding out more about innovation centers of excellence when I was planning to move from New York City, my focus was on areas full of untapped opportunity. I sought out Boston again, Silicon Valley, and Austin, Texas, and my friend David Argay, who I would later build a great business with, showed me North Carolina. Well, pass the iced tea and banjo. I may even learn to brush my tooth down there, I thought silently. But I was surprised to find a wealth of talent and resources and business down there in Raleigh Durham in the Research Triangle Park, the largest research park in the world. It was massive, untapped, and unfettered. But there were not many in the money game, venture capital, or investment-banking field who took the market seriously. (Except for a few smart and well-heeled VCs already there.) I looked all over for the facts on the four key elements of economic success in an entrepreneurial region.

1. Infrastructure
2. Technology
3. Experienced management
4. Money

I simply couldn't put my finger easily on any promotional material that was crisp and concise describing this diamond in the rough. But then, it all changed.

It became my mission—24/7—to increase the awareness of all the great things being done technically and in the venture sector in North Carolina and Research Triangle Park. I set out to educate the world and take on the establishment's existing voice and bring a new breed of resources to the region from Boston, New York, and Silicon Valley. I thought the strategy worked great and would help everyone because the pie would get bigger and more people could taste it. The rising tide would raise all ships!

I attracted and designed national and international events led by the best-of-breed technology publications in the world, *Upside* in Research Triangle Park and *Red Herring* in Atlanta. For years, I worked to blast the message of "this is a happening area" out across every medium and to anyone who would listen. I was so loud and full of piss and vinegar that eventually it actually started working. North Carolina and Research Triangle Park climbed way up on the radar screen of venture funds, investment banks, and entrepreneurs across the country, and a wave of change hit the area. I was jumping up and down on the region's waterbed. A Bill in a china shop.

However, as years of relentless ranting went on, many caught hold of the wave, many more surfed right on top of it, and even the harshest critics began to become friends. It was hard and probably impossible in another area, but as it turned out, North Carolina was on the move and the move continues to this day.

The moral of this story is simple. The world around you will fight tooth and nail and with whatever means necessary to defend its turf. You have to be willing to say "Bring it on!" The landscape is always dangerous, and you won't be able to execute if you don't understand business anthropology. It's full of predators and prey.

TACTICAL TAKEAWAYS

- Change is dynamic, fluid, and always happening—with or without your participation. Those who stand in the way of progress eventually get crushed under the weight of change.
- People, like penguins, band together when a change agent or predator is in their midst. They form a human chain and huddle together in a shivering mass only to find that is what the predator wanted—predictability, visibility, and delectability.
- If you are going to get on with getting on then you had better be ready to fight and be challenged by many along the way. If you rock the boat, no doubt some will fall out and they aren't going to like that at all.

Insider's Viewpoint

Dr. Michael O'Connor
Life Associates and The Center For Managing By Values

Studies have shown that organizations typically operate with no more than a 25 percent success rate when it comes to hiring, placing, and promoting the "right people for the right job." And, because higher performers who fit for a specific job are *not* selected, this results in higher and higher costs due to suboptimized performance, reduced capacity for utilization of management time, and further financial losses due to the eventual replacement that typically ranges from at least 3 to 10 times the annual total compensation paid to the replaced employee—in other words, an avoidable cost amounting to millions of dollars for organizations on an ongoing basis year after year. An additional study by the National Science Foundation even reported a cost of more than $100 billion per year to U.S. companies resulting from such job misfits.

Yet any organization can optimize their human capital to produce sustained and increasingly productive business results if they can overcome their own self-sabotaging practices.

Overcoming Self-Sabotaging Practice #1: The Wrong Job Requirements

The most common mistake organizations make is not being clear about the type of work results that must be produced for the organization to be more than glad to pay for the work produced by this job.

Overcoming Self-Sabotaging Practice #2: Using the Wrong Performance Predictor

The overwhelming majority of hiring decisions are based on only one factor—the candidate's job-specific capability; that is, their knowledge, skills, and

(Continued)

experience to do this specific job. But this factor alone will result in selecting performers who produce no more than average performance. Instead, high performance for jobs typically involves from two to six total performance factors . . . one of which may be this job-specific capability.

Overcoming Self-Sabotaging Practice #3: Limiting Your Organization's Success by the Obsession with Oversimplification

One of the most damaging, increasing patterns we have found is the bias among both managers and hiring professionals to "Keep It Simple, Stupid (KISS)." And, by doing so, the irony is that they make STUPID selection decisions.

Overcoming Self-Sabotaging Practice #4: Misunderstanding of the Key Drivers of Individual Performance

During the 1980s a major trend in hiring and placement of jobholders emerged. This was the competency-based approach to hiring that still is very widely used today. While it has "interesting" roots, this approach has always been fundamentally flawed. A factor that trumps capabilities (competencies) is the motivation of a person. The three types of motivations are our values (character-based performance predictor), style (personal habits—natural and learned), and interests (passions as well as disinterests). In fact, our motivations often give shape to past, current, and future capabilities that we develop, resist developing, and/or effectively put into action on any job.

There are other factors that drive success, but research shows that the single best investment that any person can make to strengthen their own chances for success in our fast-paced, changing world is to develop their personal *adaptability*. For some individuals and jobs, this involves further developing the 10 key predictors we have identified that describe individuals with high flexibility. *Flexibility* is the willingness to change and results in our increased capacity to effectively deal with adversity, ambiguity, complexity, and new situations. And, for other individuals and jobs, this requires primarily further developing a very different type of change management capacity, namely our versatility.

14

LIFE LEVERAGE

Some people can make things happen with a simple phone call. Imagine being able to call up Warren Buffett and ask for a favor you know will be granted. Bill Gates can. Social and business networking can change your life if you've worked to build a valuable network of genuinely interested associates and friends.

I've been able to build strong relationships with top industry executives in music, film, science, and technology leaders throughout the world. I hang out with some pretty cool dudes, orchestrating deals and hopefully providing a lot of value in return. But my social network gives me a lot more than the ability to name-drop. When you build your network, you should intentionally choose people who you want to do business with. You can choose to hang out with world changers, or you can hang out with detractors who don't build anything that adds value to the world. Which one will it be for you?

What are all networks, gangs, cliques, social clubs, and relationships designed for? Leverage. In life we all need a helping hand and often need leverage to overcome problems or challenges. When climbing the ladder we need a belay. In climbing, belaying is the technique of controlling the safety rope so that a falling climber does not fall very far. This task is assigned to a belayer. By using the rope properly the belayer can, with little strain, catch the full weight of the falling climber and can also help speed a climber's ascent to the next level and onward to the top of a hill. (But if you ever find me climbing a rock, I will volunteer to have my head examined.) I use this example only to point out our interdependence on one another.

In organized relationships or networks the lever is critical to getting ahead—passing a baton, getting over the wall, climbing a mountain, or simply moving up the ranks. You may try to do it alone but rarely will you ever get past first base.

The most successful leaders, entrepreneurs, intrapreneurs, and businesses have some form of organized relationship building. It's called channel development, corporate development, business development, even sales. Each player on the field has a network of contacts to sell to or align interests with, and the leadership ranks are using a strong Rolodex, always calling in favors and politicking to make sure they and their businesses forge the right alliances. This is mission critical to success in both life and business.

When is the last time you called a friend, family member, or colleague for advice, to help solve a problem, to kick the ball upfield, or to simply lean on someone's shoulder. It is a blessing, believe me, to have friends. Friends and colleagues alike use leverage to uplift one another like the Jacob's Ladder I will describe, or the various waves of the commandos and infantry. All systems and winning strategies have interdependence at their core.

A LEG UP

It's actually more like a hand up—not a handout. I have friends in high places, low ones, too. And I have been beaten down and kicked in the teeth and have done my share of beating someone's face in. But in life and business ups and downs occur and when you are up you help others come up. When you are down you hope that others will reach out and bring you up with them. It is cyclical but you never leave a man behind. That is a philosophy I have ingrained in my DNA and it has provided the edge I needed in my life, during the most insane times in deals, with people, and life's many problems. I have had more than just a leg up in life. I have been catapulted forward by some of the world's greatest minds. Relationships are important. The most well-connected people I know have a specific plan to build relationships, and often it's in writing.

DEALS ARE DRIVEN BY PEOPLE

Let's take a look at OpenSite, a company I helped put together and remained deeply involved with as a board member, once it was funded. We had leadership on the board that was strong and aligned for success. The business model and the management team were excellent. The deal had promise from the very moment the venture teams unified their networks. There were people with valuable skills in various areas to give OpenSite a leg up, not just with money but with relationships. But every business venture has challenges.

One of the challenges for OpenSite was that its business model was to enable other brands—say Sharper Image—to conduct their own auctions, not unlike eBay, but for the branded stores and products. The model depended heavily on adoption by many retailers and brands—unlike eBay, which was building a single auction clearinghouse. OpenSite used a different auction commerce model that turned out to be very successful in the wake of all the eBay attention. This was predominately due to leadership and vision, but without the various board members and the management team all rowing the boat in the same direction and bringing relationships to the table, the deal might have languished. Instead, it turned into one of the southern United States' most successful deals. Everyone was pulling his weight. It was a classic example of interdependence and the value of relationships strengthening the individuals for the benefit of the team.

Another example of leverage is Open Market. Open Market is where I met Jeff Bussgang, now an advisor to Collective IQ, who would later go on to be the founder of Upromise. Jeff was a critical leverage point for Open Market and for OpenSite. Open Market had commerce-enabling software and hooks into 30,000-plus web sites and retailers, which allowed those companies to sell products and services and bill for them. This was a leverage point for certain. If OpenSite could structure a deal with Open Market it would link the OpenSite auction technology with tens of thousands of sites and retailers overnight. You see the point there.

As in any organization seeking to leverage individuals and their skills, I was able to make contact and do the initial pitch. Once the race began I was ready to hand off the baton to the management team and, in this case, the CEO who was a rock star leader. Bang—it happened pretty darn fast! The business was on its way to forging many more similar relationships prior to being acquired by Siebel Systems for more than $400 million. It doubled after that.

Upromise is another great example of how interdependence can help a business to thrive. What a great idea. Have hundreds of thousands of retailers and product manufacturers give loyal customers pennies back on every transaction at their locations or on their products and deposit the money into a 529 plan that can be used to fund education for anyone the customer selects. People can register their credit cards and whenever they buy from a participating retailer or buy a specific product brand, a small portion of the transaction goes into the account. Social change through economic power. Even this huge idea had many interrelated dependencies.

First, in order to work, Upromise had to align with a major provider of 529 account management like Fidelity. Second, it had to go hunting for relationships with the retailers and manufacturers and convince them the program would be a great loyalty enhancement tool and a value add for their customers. The company had to get to the big boys first like Mobil, McDonald's, Coca-Cola, and so forth. Once these big brand relationships were in place, all the others would follow. This is critical and I call it the "round robin." Once you can land some big partners or brands, every other account, sale, partner, or relationship is incrementally easier to get.

Even with the traction and success of the model the team needed to scale. They had many relationships already in place, but in order to go mainstream they'd need to find a lever to massively increase exposure and customer acquisition. In all business deals you must look for the relationships one-to-one, but more importantly one-to-many, preferably thousands. In this case, the catalyst to propel Upromise to the top of the heap and into a multibillion dollar fund management business was grocery stores. As simple as it sounds the big bang came from an internal spark of brilliance to target the loyalty programs of the grocery industry. Now, that is a one-to-everyone strategy because everyone has to shop. This is yet another example of the power of relationships.

ROCKET FUEL

In the venture industry there is passive and active money. Active money plays a lead role or a more aggressive role in building the business, attracting management, forging strategic relationships among its network, and helping refine and often define key markets and business models. This is a critical differentiator. It is called value-added money. This form of capital is the greatest leverage any emerging company can get. Inside an organization the human capital is as important as the invested capital, but the leverage internally is mostly from management and the team that is attracted and the use of their relationships to advance alliances, identify channel partners, and find new business.

What propels a company forward the fastest and gets the rocket fuel into the tank is the ability to forge the one-to-many relationships. This can occur even when doing a deal where the companies collaborate on building a product or solution for the market, leveraging their resources for the common good, or cooperating on building

a technology ecostructure to leverage each other's inroads to key executives for win-win relationships. No
matter where the points of inflection are, it is critical to
move the business to new heights and away from old line
thinking that relied on a direct selling model alone. Venture capitalists and buyout funds have perfected this
model.

Business Process Outsourcing (BPO) is an example.
There are many types of outsourcing and many references
in this book about why this trend is explosive and why it
makes so much sense. It creates a symbiotic relationship
between vendors and clients that must be absolutely
flawless. The one group is highly dependent on the other
group's execution and success. If the BPO provider managing technology infrastructure, telecommunications,
telesales, in-bound customer care, and customer communications in print and electronic formats, fails to execute,
then the business is severely and adversely affected. If the
call center or data center that the business relies on for
service goes down or fails to deliver, there are potentially
hundreds of millions of dollars at risk. An Internet failure
would be a devastating blow to e-business models and
trading and interdependent systems and is always a focus
and a nightmare scenario for our cyberterrorism task
forces.

In the BPO case the provider, too, must assemble its
services and ecostructure of providers to help leverage
and execute the plan and accomplish this goal. In big
companies and small, the dependence on people and
partners is the critical factor to execution and success. It
is rare that a go-it-alone business in today's world will survive. The "not invested here syndrome" is a thing of the
past.

There is nothing more essential in the entrepreneurial world than relationships. The VCs depend on relationships with attorneys, CPAs, deal makers, friends, and associates to get access to what is called deal flow. Deal flow is the river of deals or emerging businesses that cross the desk of a venture partner. The deals roll in, and the VC processes and reviews them, looking for one out of thousands to fund. The deal is looked at from every angle: management, technology, business model, board, sales, business relationships, and so on. The VCs often compete and collaborate on deals and the tie breaker for why one VC is selected over another is his specific, powerful brand in the market.

The relationship game is critical and often focuses VCs and buyout funds into niche investment strategies because it is their *Rolodex* that is strongest in key areas and their collective wisdom in those industries that can propel a business forward so fast it would make your head spin. How many funds do you see today focused exclusively on media? Remember, content is king. There is more than $100 billion in that space alone from Veronis Sueler, Provident, Quadrangle, Elevation, and many more. Inside Texas Pacific, Blackstone, and Carlyle there are many vertical focuses and media-focused divisions. In the end, it is all about leveraging relationships to win and win fast. There is no room for organic growth anymore.

ORGANIC VERSUS INORGANIC

Organic growth can be best described as sales, sales, sales: door-to-door, direct to the customer, on the phone, plane, train, or car. It is the foot soldiering that has to be done to win business for the company. Inorganic growth often means acquisition of related businesses or competitors for their technology, people, and mostly their customers. But inorganic growth in my opinion is also the focus of corporate venture capital, corporate development, channel development, business development, and often OEM (original equipment manufacturer).

THE CHANNEL

The channel is always an interesting way to get a product to market through an interdependent relationship. It is truly symbiotic. The product manufacturers or service providers use other companies to sell and deliver their products. For example, SAP, Oracle, Microsoft—all the biggies—use value-added resellers or VARs, to extend their sales forces and technical teams to reach customers and get the product in as many companies as possible. Also, they use sales channels that again leverage their sales forces. The channel can be integrators, a critical part of major software providers, and in the enterprise resource planning (ERP) heyday every major firm from Deloitte, Accenture, EDS, Capgemini, and PricewaterhouseCoopers had armies of technology consultants customizing ERP systems, data warehouses, supply chains, and everything from the toilet to the kitchen sink. The world had become so connected and interdependent that no one company could do it alone; they all needed each other.

CORPORATE DEVELOPMENT

This role often covers inorganic growth as well. This team is responsible for a myriad of activities and much of its time is focused on acquisitions and major deal making. Most successful businesses have an absolutely, almost insane, sense of urgency to grow. They will gobble as much business, do as many deals, and grab as much of the landscape as humanly and technically possible to beat anyone to the market and own the space they are after. Companies that are heads down, focused on simply selling products and growing the bottom line are often the target of these animal companies and the corporate development maestros.

BUSINESS DEVELOPMENT

This arena is not unlike corporate development but far more partnership and alliance focused. The goal is to find as many synergistic points of leverage as possible to bring technology, products, or services into the target business alliances and to the target businesses' customers. This is critical and gets many sales or products moved fast. Companies that have stellar corporate development and business development teams are the most likely to succeed and outpace competitors. But often, the smartest companies align with external sources that play the same role but have such radically different approaches to business and relationship building, they often leave the internal teams on point A while their teams are already on Z. These catalysts are very rare—and often the winning edge if they can be used properly. Using these people and their networks is useless for simple sales.

THE STABLE

VCs and even companies rely on their stable of successful management, advisors, recruiters, and people of all sorts. Many of these trusted partners are on the lookout for all-stars to provide to companies looking for the right people. Either way, it is a network of people who are connected to deals and other people who are always looking to insert people and often want to be inserted into companies and emerging opportunities. This is one of the most critical points of leverage for investors and businesses: management.

Leverage through relationships is critical. Getting the best of breed is power. The stable is why GE has been so successful. Many GE-trained executives have gone on to run America's leading companies. It is the reason VCs turn time and time again to leaders with proven track records of success.

They deploy capital and access the stable of infantry and send them into battle to occupy a space carved out by the entrepreneur/commando. The stable or the Rolodex is the most powerful business weapon, and it will always be the best way to outpace and outmaneuver the competition. This is one of the access elements that can create velocity and acceleration.

Every deal is about people. The better your stable and management the higher the probability for success.

Like most people, I have encountered my share of management that was lazy and old school or simply not capable of running fast. Many times the difference between success and failure is to cut these people loose immediately. They are cancerous to an organization and regardless of how illustrious their public profiles may be they are simply not adequate for the task unless it is an old line manufacturing or stagnant business. Like a lot of VCs, I have also come across my share of rock stars that have won big and lost big!

HUNTERS AND GATHERERS

Nature's basic principle. Someone has to bring home the bacon and someone has to cook it. Now, one person can do both, but I think we can all agree that two heads are better than one and ten even better than that. The hunters are the commandos of business who go out and get relationships revved up and business dust flying. They plant the seeds of business growth to be harvested later by the gatherers to make food that feeds the corporation and your family. Without one, the other cannot do its job and without the pieces and parts and relationships necessary to win, most businesses will languish.

PEOPLE, PEOPLE, PEOPLE

In real estate the mantra is location, location, location. But we're talking about social and interpersonal real estate, the kind you can't get from money or property. People are the most important and most difficult elements of business and life. It is primarily people who help us succeed and cause us to fail. It's people who open doors and shut them. People are life's green lights and red lights. How many times have you heard that you can tell the character of a person by the people who surround him? Find good to great people. Treat everyone right. Reach out and help others without regard for payment or expectation of return. Shake hands and kiss babies and use every tool in the relationship shed to leverage your business. Most of all, realize you cannot do this life alone successfully.

TACTICAL TAKEAWAYS

- Relationships are the key to success. More than money, more than technology, more than management, relationships will get you where you need to go. It isn't adequate any more to go it alone. It isn't even possible to try.

- There is power in a phone call. A Rolodex is the most powerful tool in the arsenal and the most successful business executives, VCs, and entrepreneurs on earth have big ones.
- Business growth can happen in many ways but you must understand how the various roles— business development, corporate development, mergers and acquisitions, and OEM relationships—work and can work to your advantage. Not every company is really a company; oftentimes it is just a product that needs to be licensed not built out.

Insider's Viewpoint

Jeffrey J. Bussgang
Co-Founder and General Partner, IDG
Ventures Boston
Co-Founder and Former President, Upromise

Have you ever taken a meeting with someone even though you have no idea who the person is that you're meeting and why? Do you go out of your way to meet high-quality people, even if the purpose of those meetings is not initially obvious?

In today's networked business environment, it is precisely those random meetings with high-quality people that can lead to great outcomes. Although it may sound odd, you can make your own luck by seeking out and leveraging these chance meetings, and converting those you meet into valuable relationships.

Let me give you an example from my own personal history.

(Continued)

While a student at Harvard Business School, I was encouraged by one of my professors to attend a dinner that a venture capital firm was hosting. At the time, I was already planning on returning to my lucrative management consulting job after business school and frankly didn't even know what venture capital was, never mind why it would be of any interest to me. But I didn't mind meeting interesting people, and so I spent the evening with people from the firm.

That chance dinner meeting led to my abandoning my fledging management consulting career and taking a job with a young Internet commerce start-up this VC firm had backed called Open Market. This opportunity ended up being a great one for me. We went public a year after I joined, achieved a peak market capitalization of more than $2 billion, and built a market leader in a white hot space. I had the privilege of riding that wave for five years, where I got to lead many of the company's business functions, including product management, marketing, business development, and professional services.

In the middle of my time at Open Market, I got a random phone call from someone I didn't know. A VC had heard my name from somewhere and wanted to have breakfast with me. I wasn't looking for a job and didn't really have any reason to meet with this guy, but I enjoy meeting interesting people and so met him for breakfast. Another interesting person was at that breakfast—a great marketing entrepreneur named Michael Bronner. Michael had a new idea that he pitched to me: helping families save money for college by redirecting a fraction of the billions of dollars companies spend on marketing programs into tax-free college savings plans. I thought it was a brilliant idea and immediately agreed to jump on board to help found the company and serve as president and COO. Today, Upromise has over $18 billion in college savings plans under management across 8 million households in America. Sallie Mae purchased the company in 2005.

Three years into my tenure at Upromise, another VC called me. He and a friend were starting a new venture capital firm and wanted me to consider joining them. I told them I wasn't interested in becoming a VC—just like I wasn't originally interested in a job at Open Market or helping Michael Bronner start Upromise—but they were interesting people that I knew and respected, and so I took the meeting.

Fast-forward another few months, and I joined them as one of the founding general partners of a new venture capital firm, IDG Ventures Boston. We've been successful in raising and investing two early-stage funds, going on three. And now I'm the one on the other end of the phone calling up people I don't know who don't know me, and asking them to take interesting meetings that may lead to interesting outcomes.

That's what life leverage is all about. Take a few random walks, don't be afraid to explore new relationships and avenues. You never know where that next random meeting may take you.

THE SERENGETI

America was built on the principles of Aristotle. The poor, the weak, the lame would live in shacks and huts and trailer parks. The mill towns would employ them and allow entry into the city to work and do the menial tasks left for what would become the permanent social underclass in America. Not quite the Indian caste system, but close enough. Aristotle wanted the intellectuals and the elite to live within the city walls. He desired an oligarchy where the few, the rich, and the powerful ruled.

Most people, if they admit it, want to be inside those gates and are rolling diligently with the herd toward the watering hole of life trying to keep alive. But unfortunately, only a few control the watering hole and many get wounded along the way, devoured before their first drink. I see it in venture capitalism all the time. The winners win, and it's a rare one who does.

A BUSINESS SAFARI

At the first venture fund platform I helped build one of our employees showed up in my office one day. He had just had a run-in with a partner, and he was feeling a bit fragile.

"Uh, Bill, your partner just yelled at me," he said.

"Really?" I asked. "What did he say?"

"Well, he told me I screwed up some numbers and now I'm a deal killer."

"That's a shame, man," I said. "Tell you what. You go down and talk to some of the other partners and principals and then come back here."

So he set off and I could hear every pitiful moment. He wandered into various offices, telling his story. The people were working, and for the most part everyone was absolutely uncaring and waved him away. Some were on high-powered calls, orchestrating deals. The man stood in the doorways of their offices, just waiting. Eventually he came limping back to my office.

"Uh, Billy G? No one cares. They all just blew me off."

I pushed back my chair. "Okay man, let me help you out. Here you are prancing around the office toward the watering hole of life—in the most vile and ruthless of industries—the venture industry. It's the hardest to get into and the hardest to stay in. You happen to be walking along and swipe—out of an office comes a sharp paw from one of the lions, and it slices the side of your leg. You're wounded and you come limping in here and up and down the halls bleeding all over my desk and everyone else's, too. You are a little girl and if I had heels I'd make you wear them."

"Uh, Bill . . ."

"Get your bloody leg out of here, GAZELLE!" I said.

He was a colleague, and he knew my way of communicating well enough to know that what I said was true. The moral of the story is that the gazelles that get wounded and sit around thinking about it get eaten. Especially in business, and especially in a cutthroat business like investment banking or venture capital. For a long time after that, the guys in the office searched everywhere for a giant stuffed gazelle. We strung it up from the ceiling in his office. From that moment on, he was known as Gazelle.

Business should be fun. I like levity, and I like the challenges of war. In life and in business things don't always go your way. The people who survive this chaotic world and get through the peaks and troughs are battle hardened and possibly riddled with bullets. Those types don't walk away from a fight or challenge. They run straight at issues like charging lions and face them with courage and stand their ground. They fight hard and win big or lose bigger. Regardless, they come back like Rocky.

ELEPHANT HUNTING

Let's take a look at some recent developments on the Serengeti and watering hole in the high-tech world. Nintendo was an awesome game platform back in the day and everyone had one. Atari what? Then along came the Sony animals to drink from the watering hole with their PlayStation. Soon they began eating the Nintendo animals at the edges of the water and even before they ever got there. GameCube? Gone. Then comes Xbox. Who cares, right? At first the 800-pound Microsoft gorilla wasn't taken seriously at all. But then it became the new silverback that owned the gaming watering hole, and everyone was stunned.

What a fluke—NOT! Microsoft wanted to get consumers familiar with using its hardware and software products in the home and comfortable purchasing them in the stores. It was a great strategy to take over the home with the forthcoming Microsoft Home Server. And what great content Microsoft has sold to create addicts.

It's for that same reason that Dell and Gateway sell big TVs. PC manufacturers selling televisions? The PC guys realize the PC-TV will be the home interface to the world. Soon you will simply speak commands to the TV and pay for services like cable or Microsoft Office and e-mail monthly. Do you think Paul Allen was buying up all the cable for nothing?

The tundra, the largest part of the business landscape, littered with the walking dead, is the company. Not every company mind you, but then again, so many are institutionalized with old school cultures. Have you ever been in one of those environments? Grey walls with regulations posted on posters at the coffee station.

If you're not comfortable in that type of culture you may just be a maverick! Beware: The further you are from the herd the more likely you are to get hurt, bitten, and devoured. On the other hand, you are also more likely to find—or make—your own watering hole or garden. It's not about breaking all the rules; hell, it's about *making* the rules. Be the hunter not the hunted. Be the predator not the prey.

The moral of the story for adventurous entrepreneurs or executives inside a corporation who desire to be innovative, is very simple —and there are three parts.

1. You are making the game.
2. You are playing the game someone else made.
3. You are just a pawn, and who cares if you play, anyway?

THE LAWS OF THE LEADERSHIP JUNGLE

I watch deals live and die and I can tell you if you plan to go make great things happen and create dramatic wealth and opportunity you must see yourself in the mirror as larger than life. You need to be the big silverback ape that is dragging its knuckles up and down the halls of the work-place and along the crossroads of life. You have to be willing to be the one who projects yourself into the end game that doesn't even exist yet, like Bill Gates or better, Steven Jobs in his garage with his computers before he had an actual company. Confidence is the key to winning in the business jungle.

We can learn lessons from animals. If you watch lions or apes, for example, there is always one that is in charge of the pride or the clan. The big, bold male with many females and offspring is in charge and larger than life to its gang—or perhaps to employees and the world for that matter. There always comes a day, though, that the big boy is challenged. Younger, more aggressive monkeys or lions come along. They challenge the leader and the social order. Eventually the older males are beaten down by the younger, faster, and more powerful animals. They are retired in shame and their monkey family or lion's pride is taken away. Sad but true, and without a second thought for the management relics who have stayed fixed in the old ways of doing things. The fact is, leaders who get weary, who lose their confidence and their libido along the way, need to buck up, get off the decaf, and step aside—or, my best advice: Surround yourself with killers and big apes before they surround you. Don't be afraid to build a team of all-stars.

It is an endless battle of perceptions of you and the team around you that can be elevated by confidence, a can-do attitude, and a game-on winning strategy that will keep you on top of the pride.

PAINT THE PICTURE—BE THE BALL

If you do not see yourself as No. 1 in the industry or on a track to get there and declare your victories openly, publicly, and often, the PR war will be lost. Let's face it, *perception is reality* is truer than you could have ever imagined. Like a painting. It's all canvas and paint. A Monet is worth a million dollars while another lesser-known artist is worth two bucks. Same pieces and parts, but perception creates value. Why do you think YouTube sold to Google for so much? VCs had something to do with it for sure, but perception is what drove the astronomical stock value that would allow the monopoly money to flow and buy everything in its path.

THE REAL DEAL

You may have the better mousetrap and you may have a superior team, but if you can't get that message out and way above the noise level in your space, well, the other product that everyone sees will win. I cannot stress this point enough. The Silicon Valley mafia has perfected this tactic and does it so well. They drown out the competition and create such a fervor and perception of value, the next thing you know—boom!— Google goes public or Cisco buys yet another Sequoia-backed company, and so on. The rich get richer funneling deals to platforms they helped build, taking a bunch of their venture investments and merging them into the businesses they built, while the stock price is high. They know how to build businesses and value very fast and where to take the companies as they build them.

In the business jungle, have fun! Understand that some people will lift you, and some will stand in the way of your freedom and success. The next promotion, the next investor, the next piece of the business puzzle, the next partnership, and the next sale all depend on someone else you have no control over. Investing in social capital management and learning how to read people and be relational is always an investment in the future.

TACTICAL TAKEAWAYS

- The people who survive this chaotic world and get through the peaks and troughs are battle hardened and usually riddled with bullets.
- The most aggressive executives, entrepreneurs, and intrapreneurs are like charging lions that face big issues with courage. They fight hard, win big, and sometimes it's Vegas and they roll craps. No matter what, they are up again and will be until the watering hole of life is reached.
- Don't whine and take your problems to others in the ranks—save that for your social network. Do not show weakness in the office jungle; stay focused and on top of your game. Every day may be another day you act or get acted upon. Always be vigilant.
- Don't ever, ever forget that perception is reality. It has always been and always will be.

Insider's Viewpoint

Hassan Mia
Managing Partner, Keough Mia Partners
Former Managing Partner, Intel Media Ventures

The landscape in the market being described as the Serengeti is a great analogy. I have seen the best of deals come and go and the best of the best bested. It is truly deal Darwinism at its best. Only the strongest, most committed corporate leaders and entrepreneurs can survive.

Throughout my career, not only as a venture capitalist but at Creative Arts Agency (CAA), I have been in the lion's den so to speak or shark tank—in other words, the most ruthless and unkind industries on earth. But despite the competitive nature, it is truly amazing to work with some of the most creative people on earth.

I have a few suggestions for the reader who is trying to get to that watering hole: RUN! Move as fast as you can to build your ideas and business. If you don't run fast someone else will, and in fact, as soon as someone sees you sprint then there will be many more in the game, too. Also, be prepared for ups and downs, the ins and outs of the business. It's not all glitz and glamour—failure is just another way of getting something right in the end. Expect to fail.

I have been an innovator and entrepreneur—intrapreneur—most of my life and from the corporate side and external deal making side I have a view of how deals work for the intrapreneur and how differently they work for entrepreneurs. Intrapreneurs have to be in a culture where they won't be eaten alive for failure and must be given a free path to run with ideas. A culture of acceptance of new ideas, innovation, and potential failure is essential. Entrepreneurs, well they don't have a choice or safety net for the most part, and they tend to be even more desperate to win and can be much more nimble in action because they are not governed within a large organization. However, the path to success is much more risky without having a big brother or a large gorilla to help navigate the waters or the jungle—many times they are on their own and get eaten along the way.

Watch out for the dead animals and other traps on your journey; it is perilous but also most rewarding in the end—personally and sometimes financially.

16

THE WORLD IS A STAGE

Innovation leaders look at the business landscape and see the future, while most people look at the same set of conditions and see only the present. Visionaries can see what's possible and necessary before others are capable of seeing it or are ready to understand it.

Because the window of opportunity to take innovation from idea to action is breathtakingly short, innovation leaders must be able to rapidly get others on board; this means all stakeholders affected by or who may impact the success of the innovation—including customers, channel partners, employees, shareholders, and government regulators, to name a few.

The innovator's view is of the unfamiliar and it represents change. It is therefore incumbent on those leaders intent on driving innovation to develop their ability to present their viewpoint of the future in a way that others can understand, relate to, and feel compelled to support. Bottom line? You can't just be brilliant. You have to have a great idea, and you have to be a great communicator. The best innovators and most successful entrepreneurs are a combination of both. After all, how can you get your brilliant idea across to others who might be the fuel you need to birth it? No man is an island.

Earlier, I mentioned the concept of the superconnector, and how you can network in a unique way in order to help create value for others, without expecting anything in return. This concept of helping others get ahead always builds relationships, and some of the best connectors, well-liked executives and businesspeople in general, are those who have helped others in one way or another, versus simply helping themselves. Makes sense, doesn't it? It's biblical, of course, but I've found that truly the most successful people in the world are able to communicate and connect far more effectively than the average person. This concept of providing value is something that many inspirational speakers have talked about. From Tony Jeary to Keith Ferrazzi to John Maxwell, becoming a master communicator and winning with people is about perfecting the way you present your message, and communicating in a way that brings value and makes them remember you.

Tony Jeary, a worldwide motivational speaker, strategist, and coach to some of the world's top CEOs, outlines the importance of achieving what he terms "Communication Mastery." Jeary writes: "Everything in an organization revolves around communication, yet very few companies focus on it as a strategic asset to develop internally. Communication affects the way we live, talk, work, speak, write, and engage. If an organization is poor at it, or doesn't focus on it, the outcome is a poorly managed company." He goes on to explain that Communication Mastery is a methodology, a system, and a process. It's a comprehensive business strategy. Jeary teaches organizations how to present their messages better, both internally and externally. The basic foundation of his core communication philosophy is that

- People create images of influence without knowing it, each day. Images have positive and negative influence.
- Everything a leader does from a communication standpoint plays a role in creating images of influence.
- Any change that is not voluntary is not real change. If an employee's (or leader's) heart is not supportive, the results will be less than spectacular.
- Basic building blocks for strategic speed are communication and leadership.
- The primary goal of every leader is to communicate a vision effectively so that the teams can execute that vision in the marketplace.
- Mastery occurs for organizations and their leaders only when people can push through great to a higher level of mastery. Great is comfort. And when you're comfortable there is no perceived threat, and therefore no growth. *To accept great as the final destination requires acceptance of the status quo.*

THE ART OF COMMUNICATING

Presentations are the tool that innovation leaders use to influence others and enlist critical support. Any veteran of the venture industry knows how critical one presentation can be to the success or failure of an idea, an individual, or a leader.

As business leaders scan for new ways to improve performance and get a leg up on the competition, I am amazed at how easily we overlook the most promising source of improvement of all. Do you want to do more with less, achieve above average gains, increase capacity while reducing cost? Then study what the machines can teach us. We have spent decades teaching machines to mimic what humans do. We are on the verge of creating machine-based awareness. Yet here's the insight. Machines may not yet think, but they do one thing incredibly well. They communicate. Adaptors, APIs, and other interfaces allow machines of all types to talk to one another with clarity unequaled among us humans.

I've worked with Tony Jeary and have witnessed him teaching others how to present their message effectively. He has dedicated his career to helping others present their message masterfully. In his book, *Life Is a Series of Presentations*, he helps people look at all the presentations each one of us makes every day. He points out that perfectly good ideas and intentions to improve corporate performance are consistently lost to

- Misaligned performance expectations.
- Ineffective sales presentations.
- Uninspired training.
- Boring, time-wasting meetings.
- Botched media opportunities.
- Marketing communications that miss the mark.

Even more disturbing are the opportunities that are not capitalized on because they weren't even seen or recognized as opportunities. Has that ever happened to you?

I believe the next unleveraged frontier lies within our presentations. Human to human communications, on issues of importance, have fallen behind that of machine to machine communications in terms of clarity, efficiency, and effectiveness. With the exception of some technical and scientific areas, structured interfaces for human to human communications haven't been well defined, and disciplined use of interface protocols are limited. Bottom line is that most human to human interchanges are almost completely unstructured and are susceptible to high variability, which means they carry a high risk of failure.

From what I've observed in entrepreneurial ventures, some people achieve far greater success than most because they have discovered a way to reduce variability and risk. They reap enormous benefits simply by being effective in their presentations virtually every time—whether scheduled and rehearsed or ad hoc.

In our attention deficit society our ideas are in constant competition with other ideas and agendas. Squandering even innocuous opportunities can spell the difference between success and failure; the difference between fast and efficient or slow and wasteful.

How does it work?

Jeary says that master presenters really know their stuff inside strategically defined presentation domains, and they know not to wander outside those boundaries. Establishing a presentation domain means defining

- Who you need to reach (audiences).
- What you want to talk about (topics).
- What you want to communicate (predetermined key messages).
- What you want people to do as a result (objectives).
- How you want to be perceived in the process (image and style).

Second, communication masters make it a strategic priority to organize their presentation resources and manage both preparation and delivery of presentations in a disciplined way. They efficiently access a presentation arsenal (mental, hardcopy, and electronic) that provides ready access to appropriate resources, methods, and techniques for use during both their preparation and delivery.

Finally, the best presenters know that mastery is a temporary state, and in reality is a journey instead of a destination. They continue to hone their skills and reach for more aggressive goals.

Communication is something that most sales organizations focus on, yet you won't find it a high priority within the upper echelons of leadership or departments like finance or innovation. Communication and the way we present our individual and corporate messages is seen as a function of marketing, sales, or branding. But in this technology-driven era we live in, communication will rise up to be an even greater asset among world-class companies. As we all become extremely accustomed to more and more online and written communication, the way we interact face to face and the skills we each need to develop to become excellent communicators and presenters in front of audiences, need refining.

Most organizations now communicate virtually wholly with the written word—in short bursts, words, and sentences. The Crackberry sleeps by the bedside and the killer app should be pajamas and a pillow for it. The always-on e-mail, instant messaging, and corporate portals have stepped in front of, and for the most part made it unnecessary for, person-to-person communication.

In the past, communication would take the form of one person entering another person's office to have a full conversation about a client. Today, the communication looks something like this:

> Tom,
> XYZ Corp wants to cancel its contract with no penalty. Need approval.
> Bill
>
> B, Not possible.
> Tom.

Our communication attention span has compressed, just like everything else in society. We talk faster, in shorter sentences, and listen less. We do it with friends, family, and business associates, sometimes brokering millions of dollars of deals with a simple text message. I know people who have sold a product worth thousands in two simple e-mail exchanges. Imagine that a decade ago! Selling poolside, with your BlackBerry.

The point is that as our communication evolves—or devolves—becoming an excellent, and perhaps even a master communicator, can truly set you apart. In a world of whatevers and informal abbreviated text messaging terms, people with the ability to succinctly and intelligently articulate their messages and sell themselves and their concepts, will reign.

TACTICAL TAKEAWAYS

- The age-old saying is true: "You only have one chance to make a first impression." In business, and especially in the venture capital business, this is dead-on.

- Get help. Ask for advice from leaders and find winning presentations out there. Hire a coach and perhaps an image advisor. Use advisors and writers and professionals in every industry to get your message across properly. Get your game on.
- Get to the point. People often underestimate their audience when giving a pitch or speech. Understand your audience and be crisp and clear.

Insider's Viewpoint

Tony Jeary
Coach to the World's Top CEOs

I like to think my methodology is unique, in that I've studied the best practices and habits of highly successful people for decades, and now I apply those principles and behaviors to my own life and business, and that of my clients as well. I help people present better, because I truly believe that we make presentations each and every day, in every aspect of our lives. I try to help clients understand that we are always presenting—even if it's with friends, family, or loved ones. What's the message you have to get across? How will you influence the recipient?

Achieving goals faster, with speed and clarity, is an important distinction between the top companies today and the rest of the pack. I help guide companies and their CEOs get results faster, through strategic clarity and Communication Mastery. This helps people execute their visions, which Billy G talks about in this book. Sometimes it means doing things differently and taking a left on red. As a coach to some of the world's top CEOs, I can testify that most high achievers do things differently. My clients have included normal people like you and me, as well as the presidents of Ford, Samsung, New York Life, Firestone, and Sam's Club. Each of these special people has a distinction about the way they do business, and my own personal distinction has been a devotion to giving value and doing more than is expected, which is my life mantra. What does that mean? It means I'm willing to be different, and do more—in order to help others achieve the clarity they need, and the results they want, faster.

You have to be really clear on where you want to go, and how you'll get there, in order to achieve your destiny.

IDEATION: THE NEW ECONOMY FUEL

Ideas. Everyone has them.

Some have them more frequently than others and some are able to act on them, executing brilliantly. Still others are veritable think tanks of ideation yet seem to execute almost nothing. In the venture industry and perhaps in yours as well, you meet people like that all the time—people with half of an idea, or even a half-baked entrepreneurial venture, who simply can't get all the resources, or parts and pieces to fit together to create something significant.

The difference between those who talk about things and those who execute is vast. Building a new idea into a business takes innovative thinking, chutzpah, and a lot of determination—among about 50 other things! Energy to endure is first and foremost.

Where do ideas come from?

Sometimes the best ideas evolve from someone else's idea that never got hatched. This happens all the time, when someone builds a better mousetrap or is able to execute a specific add-on or add an innovative concept to a preexisting idea. There are thousands of examples of that. Take, for example Crocs and the little Jibbitz buttons that were invented and added on to the plastic shoes—as if making millions from colorful plastic shoes wasn't a great enough invention already. Or take Google, a business built on top of the preexisting information already available out there in cyberspace, or online gaming, poker, and interactive game sites, and the multitude of innovations appearing each day out of the long since birthed Internet. No doubt, the Internet is where it's at, but ideation can be anywhere. You don't need to be a techno genius to crack the code of entrepreneurship and come up with a world-changing idea.

I've found that the best ideas come when you give yourself and your mind the space to think. Sure, sometimes it's a requirement to think fast and have flashes of brilliance appear on a moment's notice when critical decisions need to be made.

It's important to be able to call on an array of mental resources in a meeting, with multiple attendees, conversations, and arrows coming your way. But sometimes the best ideas come when you are alone in the wilderness, either figuratively or actually, when your mind and body have the highest amount of energy for them. In a culture where we are all so focused on time and achieving the greatest amount in the shortest time frame, sometimes our calendars are so jam-packed that it is nearly impossible to free up the energy required for ideation.

MIND POWER AND THE BIRTH OF AN IDEA

In his book *Chasing Daylight*, Eugene O'Kelly, the CEO of KPMG, wrote about how his perspective and ideas changed after he stepped into his doctor's office with a full calendar and a lifetime ahead and was diagnosed with terminal brain cancer. A high achiever with an abundance of ideas, contacts, and appointments, O'Kelly determined in the end that the best use of his mind in the 100 days he had left on earth, (in addition to writing a book!) was to control energy, instead of time. The notion of controlling energy would mean to be in pursuit of greater balance by intentionally deploying the methods of world-class athletes and making improvements in physical and dietary habits, sleeping well, and setting aside quiet, meditative time for reflecting and training the mind.

Most of us get too caught up in the day-to-day to step back and understand what's working and what's not with regard to how our individual energy is depleted, or increased, but it's worth thinking about. What if, by evaluating this one thing, you could increase your ideation, energy flow, and effectiveness?

Here is a cool example. One day a friend of mine and I were jacked on Caribou Coffee getting my jet skis tuned up. Dave was helping me, and we were enjoying the time together. It was downtime, fun time, time to reflect. We weren't thinking about business, particularly, just enjoying life and getting energized from each other. But fun bleeds over into business, and often it's the downtimes we learn from and incorporate into our professional lives.

Dave and I raced down the road in the car. He pointed to a tree and said:

"Hey man, look at that tree—it's a leaner."

"What the *blank* is a leaner?" I asked.

"It's a tree that's leaning over and likely to hit a house."

"So what?"

"Well," he replied, "leaner trees cause several issues. Look at how close it is to falling on their house."

I looked. Sure enough, the tree looked as if it could topple at any minute.

"If I could go to estate properties, and remove the leaner trees, the homeowners could call their insurance company to drop their rates."

Yeah right, I thought. I just spent three years creating a new asset class called the "collateralized private equity obligation." We spent years building a database to convince reinsurance and rating agencies about the probability and volatility of venture capital; nonliquid investment that we helped the market understand in order to forecast liquidity. So I felt I had a bit of background in understanding insurance.

When we reached my home in Raleigh, David pointed out a Japanese maple tree that had been transplanted from the backyard.

"See that tree?" he said. "That tree would cost more than $7,500 to replace."

"Ha-ha. Yeah right." A stick and leaves. It was there when I bought the place.

"No man, seriously. That maple is at least $7,500 without labor if you had to just buy the silly tree."

Later on I found myself climbing up over the iron fence to move lighting away from the leaves so the tree wouldn't get singed. What had happened? My perception changed. I called my insurance agent and he said that there was no such thing as landscaping insurance. He told me I would get $250 per plant if something happened such as a fire, a storm, or a flood under my existing policy. Well, the fact is there isn't one plant, except maybe flowers, in my yard that would cost less than $1,000 (not including labor) to replace. And that is this year. What about next year, when it has grown bigger and will be more expensive to replace?

From that moment of downtime with my friend Dave, a new business was born. After that initial conversation I went online and typed in the URLs landscapeappraisal.-com, landscapeappraising.com, landscapeinsurance.com, and so on and on and on. Then I took a cybertrip to the U.S. Patent and Trade Office to do a search on landscape appraising. Nothing. I mean seriously, someone had to have thought of landscape appraising and insurance or the value of curb appeal? Nothing. Absolutely naked space.

Okay, so break out the Mountain Dew and darts. David and I spent the next three days without sleep, a shower, or a shave. He was a landscape genius—that's his business, and I learned the industry inside out. I learned about the players in the industry, the various components of the supply chain, and everything I could learn about plants. Once the weekend was over we had written our plan and first thing Monday morning we were on the way to an intellectual property law firm to slap $100,000 down. We hired actuaries in London, and my partners in Colorado worked on the framework and patents.

Then we went out for a brand. What will we call this thing? We finally bought a URL from a hack—www.moneygrowsontrees.com. We set out to become the Kelley Blue Book for installed landscaping and to create landscaping appraisals, insurance, and warranties. We went extremely large, okay, over the top, and secured more than 700 nurseries to buy in as well as all of the Green Industry Associations, the major arborist companies, landscape architects, tens of thousands of realtors, and the major insurance companies.

What we found, essentially, is that through ideation we could solve a very real problem. The $100 billion aggregating supply chain forgot to pick up its value chain. Essentially the value of the plants stopped once they were installed at a property. We went out and knocked on all our friends' doors and ended up raising several million dollars, mortgaging our houses, and tossing and turning all night long for a few years before our baby was born.

Color Cut Clarity = Hardiness Habit Growth Rate and Color. How's that for an easy way to explain it? You try to figure out how thousands of plants grow and grow differently in each zip code! A Japanese maple in Raleigh, for instance, grows differently than it would in Florida—compared to Minnesota where it would die. It was virtually one of the only uninsured—or underinsured—assets in the world. Hell, if I can insure my dog that I got for free, I should be able to insure $100,000 of landscaping! I can't walk out of a Best Buy without a warranty being shoved in my hand for an electronics purchase. Here's what we wrote as an overview of the company right out of the chute, and it was dead-on, and hasn't changed much since.

Overview

HMI is seeking to pursue what its management team and advisors believe is a significant nascent opportunity in the U.S. horticultural and real estate marketplace to measure, value, and insure the current and future replacement cost of horticultural assets.

Currently, existing appraisal services, software, and valuation methodologies do not have measurement tools, statistical information, pricing or valuation metrics focused on evaluating the annual "investment" being made by consumers into structural and horticultural modifications to real estate. Nor can they capture the existing value of prior investments or, in the case of plant material, the vast inventory of pre-existing mature specimens. This represents a significant market opportunity. It is estimated that U.S. consumers purchase more than $7 billion per year in new plant material. Add that to what pre-exists and it is clear that HMI's applications can release 100s of billions of dollars in stranded assets across the country. Once valued, these assets become candidates for a wide array of financial services, such as insurance, warranties, and financing.

Roughly 7.6 million home sales occurred in 2006. Of this number 1.1 million were new homes and 6.5 million were existing home sales. Currently, an appraisal is required for the vast majority of these transactions. In addition, for a growing number of closings, a house inspection is also required. These products provide the consumer, lending institution, and insurer with confidence in both the valuation and condition of the property being acquired. Neither product addresses what is a significant asset on the majority of those properties—the landscaping and mature trees. HMI feels that the addition of a horticultural asset inspection and valuation would be a significant value-add to these transactions and would create substantial economics for the financial services companies and green industry suppliers who participate in this supply chain.

HMI, in alliance with horticultural industry expert Dr. Michael A. Dirr, various associations, and large industry partners, has assembled the world's largest commercial repository of scientific and economic data for licensed appraisers, landscape architects, landscape contractors, arborists, and horticulturists to use to capture the "real" asset value that exists on commercial and residential properties across the country. HMI's patent-pending standard is the first measurement system that couples value with that knowledge and delivers it directly to the consumer through a trained professional. HMI believes that this will increase substantially the appreciation of the horticultural workforce, their value proposition, and the amount invested by consumers.

Ideation at its finest. And all from a fun day spent with a friend. We were energized just by being together, tuning up the jet skis, bouncing ideas off of one another, and making observations about the world.

THE NEXT BIG THING

If you find yourself pondering a great idea, get it down on paper. Do your research with the U.S. Patent and Trade Office for what's called "prior art," which is an idea that has already been patented. Hire an attorney to put together a company you can park your idea into and get started writing a business plan. I have written hundreds and raised hundreds of millions of dollars for companies. You can do it, too.

Maxine Clark, the founder of Build-A-Bear Workshop, made millions with her idea to open stores that allow kids to make, dress, and name teddy bears! She took the company public, and it became a behemoth venture, all birthed from a simple idea. Hey, let's take a stuffed animal and make a business by dressing it up as a cheerleader, or a football player with the favorite local team, or a firefighter, or anything else a child could want. Brilliant! A bigger and better and more personalized mousetrap, for sure.

It's never easy birthing a dream, no matter how big the idea or how small. Money Grows on Trees was an awesome concept but it wasn't easy, even if I make it sound like a cakewalk. It got harder along the way, and we dealt with a variety of issues. Management personalities are always the most difficult to deal with in any business, and with that one we had to make payroll while the leadership ran out of money six times. Talk about pressure! We were vigilant and after three years of building, finally surrounded ourselves with a great team, a fabulous board, and a wealth of smart advisors. All that, and we had just reached the starting line. I did mention perseverance before, didn't I?

What's your big idea?

You're never too old or too anything to come up with one. It may be something that's been percolating inside of you for the last decade or some kernel of thought that someone planted in your mind years ago that's been germinating. The crossroads of your life experience has been building, and maybe now you've got the right amount of energy and horsepower to make it happen. Go for it!

TACTICAL TAKEAWAYS

- Ideation can happen to any of us. We all have dreams and ideas. The difference between living a life of quiet desperation and living your dream is mostly showing up for the game.
- No matter how you look at it, creating a company will be difficult. Drink lots of coffee or Mountain Dew.
- Management, management, management! Surround yourself with the best team and advisors, take as much money as you can, and run as fast as possible and always get great attorneys to protect your intellectual property.

Insider's Viewpoint

Naveed Khan
Co-Founder, Siemens Ventures,
Executive Director of the Strategic Venture
Association

The foundation of any good business or product begins with an idea. The entrepreneur, intrapreneur, or product developers have to be able to think where no box exists. There can't be any red lights to impede their work flow. Red lights simply slow the process and can be devastating to the idea. Ideation is delicate and a talent not everyone will have or needs to have. Any idea that is to be turned into a product or business will require a collective team of various talents coming together to make it successful.

When I was running Siemens Ventures, we saw ideas coming at us internally from the labs and externally from various deal sources. The ideas were incredible but it took much more than that. Many had great slideware and a slick pitch but really were only ideas at the time. In order to attract capital and bring an idea beyond the incubation period you must have several elements assembled before you are ready to go for professional or strategic funding.

1. Product. Not just an idea or prototype—unless it is a truly revolutionary working prototype.
2. Management. A team must surround the idea and product. You need advisors, a board, management —preferably management that has been successful before, although this can be built out by your venture partner.
3. Market. You have to have a defined market and a product that fits. It must fill a need.
4. Sales. The early adopter and first sales are critical to validating the technology and its viability. Venture capital has moved upstream to funding later stage deals.
5. A big deal. Do not be shy. If you think your deal is big, then make the case and win the argument.
6. Perseverance. Regardless of how long it takes, or how bad it gets, get your idea to market.

18

TAKE THE WHEEL

What makes a company red versus green? Some people are inclined to ask, "Who the hell knows?" Someone hugged a tree and a group cranked out Earth Day, and you can bet your corporate vision will now include a green strategy and the world will never be the same. Business has gone green. It's a movement that motivates consumers to buy and helps the world at the same time.

General Electric decided to drop all its eggs right into the green basket with renewable energy, energy efficient appliances, lightbulbs, and even aircraft engines that are better for the environment. The whole company turned on a dime and years ahead of everyone else. Today, we'd call it going green, but I call that going left. Sometimes, a leader has to be willing to step away from what everyone else in the industry is doing just to do what seems right.

Jeffrey Immelt, 49, the heir to the Jack Welch regime, is a Left on Red thinker building a Left on Red company. Balls to the wall, jump without a net, and innovate the crap out of things or as a *Business Week* article recently stated, "His fear is if he doesn't GE will become a boring company and risk losing great executives because of the sheer bottom-line-only focus."

So what makes the difference? What makes one person stand out in an organization, or one company break away from the pack while the rest follow?

FIRST THINGS FIRST

Entrepreneurs are born and not necessarily trained. They may have training that can help them refine their skills but frankly, you either have it or you don't. It is all about DNA, which means that most leaders are innovators and mavericks.

There are thousands of students attending school and taking courses in entrepreneurship and management while others dropped out of school to become entrepreneurs and build companies that they manage. I'm not advocating becoming a dropout. Learning is essential. But there are two kinds of leaders.

One kind of leader goes through the system and actually becomes a great leader, but the talent was within them the whole time or else the corporate animals would have eaten them long ago. The other kind bends and breaks rules of nature, society, and industry and reinvents things the way they see it and a whole new kind of ice cream, or software, or even chicken sandwich emerges.

A WINNING CULTURE

A business culture is a society within a workplace. Some are like the plantations of old with slave labor tightly held under the thumb of literal tyrants like Mr. Potter from *It's a Wonderful Life*. I have seen it, and it's disturbing at best.

Other business cultures are loosey-goosey with no direction at all, zero inspiration, and a come-and-go as you please environment. The standouts are game on, coffee flowing, high energy, no backstabbing or politics allowed cultures like SAS, Molson Coors, and a lot of others managed by great leaders.

These cultures are built inside companies that inspire people at all levels. There is no air of superiority and entitlement among leadership.

What kind of culture are you working in? What kind of culture do you hope to help build and cultivate? Every individual at any level who is part of a working team or organization has a significant role in building the culture. The words we say, and the choices we make either build or destroy. It's the same with your family, by the way. In your own home you are building a mini-culture, and the attitudes you bring to that culture help build or destroy. Life mirrors business and business mirrors life.

I know you have looked in the mirror many times. But I bet you hardly ever really looked in the mirror at yourself. I don't mean your face or eyes or lips—but you—who you are, what you are doing, and where your life is at this very moment. Many of us are afraid to ask these types of questions and only glance at ourselves from time to time to make sure our hair is combed or there isn't food stuck on our teeth. You need to think about who you are, not who you think you are. Self-awareness is a huge part of the equation and any success guru, consultant, or high achiever will tell you that. There are different ways to gauge your self-awareness, and when it has been measured accurately the real journey of growth and development can begin.

Start by evaluating yourself against three types of people:

1. Those making it happen.
2. Those watching it happen.
3. Those it is happening to.

Becoming more aware of the times when you're making things happen versus how often others are dictating the events in your life is an important and life-defining distinction. It's a moment to stop the hustle and take stock of your social and economic position. It's a time to figure out where you rank among the pack of humans in your clique, office, or gene pool. The hardest part—and it is this way for all of us, is to be completely honest no matter what the circumstances.

Are you a big gorilla or a monkey? Polar bear or penguin? Commando or police officer? Come on now! Not everyone can be a predator and ride shotgun every time. The truth is that in life there aren't enough window seats to go around. Most people just aren't predators; they're prey, not a full-fledged hunter just yet. In our animal kingdom, across the vast business tundra, the weak get eaten and the aggressive are never hungry. Even if you think you are a big gorilla, remember there are monkeys growing up around you every day.

YOUR LICENSE TO DRIVE

The only way you can come up with the wrong answer in a self-assessment is if you lie to yourself. It is a simple fact that whoever you are, wherever you are, or whatever you are, the cards you have in your hand are those you have to play. Regardless of what hand life dealt you and any mis-plays along the way, it is what it is. Some people have a hard time with self-assessment because it will most certainly lead to change. Change is hard to wrap your arms around when life is as busy as it is these days. Cole Peterson, the former HR director for Wal-Mart, managed the largest group of associates in the world. Throughout his career he encouraged people to continually do self-assessments to en-hance self-awareness.

In particularly cutthroat industries, like investment banking, real estate, or venture capitalism where competi-tion is high and sharpness a requirement, you can't afford to have a false perception of your ally, your enemy, or yourself. With colleagues and partners I stress thorough-ness and honesty and becoming comfortable in their own skins. Establishing a baseline for our lives and a solid foundation to build upon is important in order to have a clearly defined starting point. Without knowing exactly where you stand you will never be able to use any book, compass, or map to get out of the woods and safely on the way to life's watering hole. You can't get where you are going if you don't know where you are. And remem-ber, whatever got you here won't get you there!

There are three qualities of the most on fire, Left on Red thinking visionaries that I have ever encountered in business.

1. They are self-aware, not delusional.
2. They leverage their social capital, through life and business networks.
3. They know that first and foremost, knowledge is power and imagination even more powerful. They thirst for knowledge, information, and ideas, and

always seek to leverage others' contacts, business acumen, and time toward a common good.

THE POWER OF SELF-APPRAISAL

Take stock of your business and your role in it. First understand the business itself and where it fits into the overall market. Understanding the business organism and dissecting it into its pieces and parts provides further knowledge of how everyone contributes to the organization. Who runs things and who runs from things? Who is aggressively on the move or politicking up the ladder? This appraisal is very important. You'll need a map of the organization in order to make things happen and avoid pitfalls and also to find external or internal allies that can add value to your network.

In order to develop outside connections and meet influencers critical to your success or business it's important to understand the working parts and to be able to identify areas where you can add value and contribute beyond your present responsibilities.

Throughout the appraisal process you should identify inflection points, inefficiencies, or failures within the four walls that can be brought to your network to uncover best practices or ideas and to challenge your own ideas. This takes intellect to understand issues, access to leaders or influencers, and even colleagues to collectively come up with ideas and strategies.

Building a collective IQ is as it sounds: a collection of people who are unified for each other's common good. This power base can act as a fulcrum in life, a point of leverage that can move large obstacles or mountains if need be. This becomes an arsenal of wisdom in your revolutionary war. Your social network determines your life's net worth. It's something the most successful people in the world build on.

"It's not what you do, it's who you know!"

Joel Katz is a perfect example of this age-old adage. Joel, a superconnector, did quite a bit of mentoring for me and I have spent years sitting in an office right next to him. Princes, kings, politicians, and captains of industry would call Joel every day. He could pick the phone up at any moment and speak with the chairman of ABC, NBC, Time Warner, or almost anyone he needed to across the world. On many occasions, Joel introduced me to executives and influencers at all levels—CEOs of record labels, the president of Live Nation, the chief marketing officer of Coca-Cola, the chairman of Nokia, and the CEO of Cendant before he became CEO of Realogy (Century 21, ERA, Coldwell Banker). It is good to have friends in powerful places. They can help you get things done.

Relationship currency is more valuable than money. In the end, you can always make money with relationships but money won't always buy you the value that can come with relationships well tended.

One of my holding company's board members is a powerful man voted one of the 25 most powerful people who help America win. He also runs the Royal Institution World Science Assembly that Peter Norton and I helped fund and support. I asked Dan for introductions for Money Grows on Trees, and he made one phone call and there I was in front of Hank Greenberg, former Chairman of AIG, who liked the business and then called the vice chairman of Chubb to kick things off. What an honor to have such a powerful business icon spend time with you and reach out to help. Your network is your largest asset, and it might be one phone call that can create millions of dollars of value in minutes.

How does one create a collective IQ? It's not easy, but the major players know how to do it. Those who aren't there yet have not developed the people skills or extroverted personality to forge this network. The latter will have to find inflection points created by other people and then plug in. Young Presidents Organization is just one example of a network already established that can help serve many of the needs of advancement. The local Rotary Club is another way of connecting where wisdom and relationships can be shared. Any organization with leverage and business intelligence can help you grow.

It's important to form a network outside your organization to become more powerful within it. This network—no matter how big or small—is a great support group to provide wisdom and advice while constructively challenging your way of thinking. It took me years of cold calling and looking up executives only to be blown off. To my surprise many people were interested to learn more about opportunities for themselves and where they could potentially use their positions to improve their business and their social network. People are generally selfish. The more you can do for others, the better it will be for your own life and business. This is called the law of reciprocity! Do things for others selflessly and don't expect something in return. They won't be obligated to return the favor, of course, but you're building your collective IQ along the way and they'll remember you when it counts. No matter how you make the connections—make them.

CONNECTING THE DOTS

When recruiting others to join your network, get away from your comfort zone and seek groups, individuals, and perhaps companies that are clearly synergistic to your business or division or that seem to be able to add value toward developing future connection points that can help your next move up. The best network is the one you build.

Those at the helm, the top of the organizational heap, have large Rolodexes. They have built relationships over time and as they grow the relationships grow with them. Their Rolodex advances them and they advance those in the Rolodex.

Be aware, though, of takers. Takers take. No matter how many favors you do or how many times you help them, or whatever you do to connect them to others, they will simply take anything they can get from you and never give back. Identify people and personalities and only surround yourself with others who can uplift you and who you can uplift. Like a Jacob's Ladder, the electricity only flows if there is a connection between the left and right and the current in between linked together. Let's call this harmonizing humans or globally harmonizing humanity. All for one and one for all.

NURTURING THE NETWORK

Great connectors and networkers don't expect anything from their network. They are usually the ones "paying it forward" and doing good things for good people.

This brings people closer to you and they see you as a value-added component of their networks. Soon you are networked into their networks and the base of relationships grows. Seek a microphone. If you can get yourself into a position to speak to groups of people, that's a great way to provide them a glimpse of yourself while recruiting many of them into your network. Once you have just a few relationships to leverage, capture knowledge nuggets and use them in your journey to the top.

AVOIDING A CRASH

Ah! Hope lies within. Each one of us, big or small, wise or imprudent, has much to gain from the simple principles of Left on Red thinking. Most would describe this as a contrarian point of view, paddling upstream or going against the grain. And in fact it is. In order to navigate the waters or climb the tree you must first see the fruit at the end of the branch. Seeing the fruit is simply a metaphor for knowing what rewards come with taking risks, the direction to take to get there, how fast you can climb, and being prepared to fight to reach it.

The best way to avoid a crash or getting beaten in a food fight is to leverage the collective wisdom of others. Finding others who are successful and have had deep and meaningful struggles in life and business is critical if you ever plan to break some rules and avoid crashes along the way. These people can save you a lot of headaches and trips to societies' various jails. Their knowledge is power.

STOP! THE LIGHT IS RED

Stand up! Sit down! Lose weight! Buy, buy, buy. Why? Because we told you to! Don't rock the boat. Don't run through your life with your hair on fire. And by all means, don't think for yourself. Follow the herd and you won't get hurt or get in trouble. Boy, what a life—the American Dream. Really?

The big thing some inspirational speakers push these days is total life balance, but some of the best lives are completely unbalanced much of the time. Do you think the Google guys, Sergey Brin and Larry Page, had balanced lives during the time they were masterminding the company that would change the world, or do you think they had a few sleepless nights and weeks on end?

I've observed many successful entrepreneurs go through gallons of Jolt cola and Mountain Dew jacked to the hilt on Starbucks, all the while becoming regulars in marital and family counseling, and I can attest that my name is Bill Glynn and I am a deal junkie, workaholic, and outright off my rocker. Am I balanced? Ha! Many entrepreneurs and big hitters go around the clock, every day of every week, driven, no compelled, to bring their vision to life and their lives are anything but regulated and nothing less than organized chaos.

I have witnessed entrepreneurs go from two people in a garage to 1,000 employees in 12 to 18 months. Does that seem like a normal experience?

I have seen people who had to scrape change out of their cars to get some gas become billionaires. I have seen some make hundreds of millions of dollars only to be bankrupt the next year. Normal? Unbalanced? Chaotic? You bet! And I would say with confidence it is just the way it is when you have become what I gladly call unemployable.

I have lived on the inside of many companies and have worked closely with many entrepreneurs and executives having built Excite and Match Logic, Open-Site, Red Storm Entertainment, BuildNet, Upromise, Red Hat, and many more. I have had talks around the table and in the green room with Bill Wrigley, Tom Siebel, Marc Andreessen, John Chambers, Tom Peters, Tim Sanders, Tim Draper, Hollywood icons, heads of nations, Nobel winners, musicians, and record executives. No matter what company, bought, sold, bankrupt, or public, no matter at what scale and how international the personality, common traits were always evident.

Drive, almost insatiable ambition, a relentless pursuit of excellence, an unshakable vision, and confidence in themselves and their acceptance of nothing less than personal or professional victory. They all seemed to embody an attitude of triumph and perseverance, actually more like an instinct, which under any circumstance—even the most adverse and severe—would allow them to rise while others, even the best of us, would mentally collapse and hide under a desk. Nothing! No barrier. No system. No one would ever be able to stand in their way.

To climb so high, so fast, to become so recognized the world over does throw one's life into a blender at first and often it stays on high speed. Unbalanced, eccentric, out to lunch would be very good words to use to describe some of the most successful people, because they are so committed to what they have built or become, it simply becomes a dominant part of who they are. However, in my personal and professional experience, it is this rare breed of visionary, high-octane executive, entertainer, or entrepreneur who frankly wouldn't trade one second of their hectic often-chaotic lives for anything. Their deals, companies, vision, and talent are simply their art, the world their canvas, their minds the brush.

The majority aren't like the example above, building on momentum and turning Left on Red when needed. Most people glide along a path in life and are stopped by many a red light along the way. Dead stop! Life's momentum and upward mobility are halted and after awhile the simple act of stopping and starting just wears one down, and before you know it the car is pulled over and there you sit in life's parking lot, dream abandoned. Red lights are everywhere.

THE DANGER OF YIELDING

The battle to control your destiny, to win your right to be free from conformity and to climb the tree and grab some tasty fruit will come with adversity, failure, and hard knocks along the way. The glass ceiling exists. The fact is, fear causes hesitation and hesitation causes your worst fears to come true. Most people won't dare run the red light or even turn quickly down another path because of conditioning and fear. If you are to become an innovator, a game changer, or game maker, shedding those fears, running red lights, or cranking a turn when needed is the only way to do it.

LIGHT AT THE END OF THE TUNNEL

Viktor Frankl is a powerful example of human perseverance, deep insight, and profoundly grounded self-awareness and social truth. His experience in the Nazi concentration camps would rank No. 1 on the most vile, terrifying, life-altering experiences one could ever face. Having his own family exterminated and living through a horrifying experience, he went on to write *Man's Search for Meaning*, one of the 10 most impactful pieces of literature in human history. Throughout his ordeal, he observed that of those given a chance for survival, it was only those who held onto a vision of the future, who longed to see loved ones, to build a new life from ashes, to see freedom, that were most likely to survive their suffering. His words ring true today for all of us. "You can't always choose your circumstance but you can choose your attitude." Once you clearly see yourself in that mirror and can visualize a powerful future for yourself, only then do you have any chance of making it across the intellectual desert and surviving the inevitable war you will fight in order to win your right to succeed.

You shall know the truth and the truth shall set you free.

TACTICAL TAKEAWAYS

- Entrepreneurs and mavericks are born. Training can develop great leaders and the system can offer some training, but the most successful go around the system.
- Take the wheel of life and drive! Don't wind up in the backseat or worse—the trunk.
- Adopt a positive outlook even in the most vile of situations. It's a life-changing strategy to let as much as you can roll off your back.
- Fear causes hesitation. And hesitation causes your worst fears to come true!

Insider's Viewpoint

Barry Landis
30-Year Music Executive and One of the Top 25
Influencers in the Christian industry
Former President of Warner Music Group Label
Word Records

Our legacy is all we leave behind in the end. For
many, the family they created becomes their legacy;
for others their good works. For a very few their foot-
print is firmly planted in the sands of time.

Nobel for certain left his mark, and we recognize
others today leaving their marks on society through
Radnor's ability to extend Nobel's accomplishments
into a lasting vision. I have always thought in terms of
legacy. It is important to think of yourself and how
you will be remembered in 100 years. We only live
once and you want to make it count for something.

If you think in terms of legacy it can help shift
your perception outward and stretch the fabric of your
life beyond mortality, and that for certain will change
the way you spend your short time on earth. Perception is one of the only things about yourself that you
can change, and your attitude toward circumstances
both good and bad can change the way you live your
life. These facts and human laws govern our state of
mind from day to day and year to year, and the profound influence of Viktor Frankl lives on today and
should be ingrained in all of our souls.

If I can add one verse to Billy G's work, if I can ever
get a word in edgewise it would be this: Follow simple

(Continued)

rules in life, take each day as a new opportunity to be someone you always dreamed about being, don't let anyone or anything stand in your way and always cherish the moments in your life. It is the moments woven together that become our life. Unfortunately, most of us let them slip through our hands like sand in an hourglass.

"Life is just what happens to you, While you're busy making other plans."

—John Lennon

ON BECOMING A STUDENT OF INNOVATION

DR. DENIS WAITLEY

As the world becomes more interconnected, events outside your industry and career have an impact on your business, your family, and your pocketbook. Whatever your daily routine, it takes place in a larger context of social, technological, political, economic, and cultural change. To be successful today, you must understand that world. Without that you won't be prepared to innovate; you'll only be able to react and to avoid.

Many people will tell you it doesn't matter how well-informed you are. "You can't do anything about it anyway," goes the refrain, "so why bother to find out about things?" Here's a newspaper editorial that sums up this attitude:

The world is too big for us. Too much going on, too much crime, violence and change. Try as you will, you get behind in the race. It's an incessant strain to keep pace and still you lose ground. Science empties its discoveries on you so fast that you stagger beneath them in hopeless bewilderment. Everything in business and life is high pressure. Human nature can't endure much more!

This newspaper editorial reads as if it were written last week. But it actually appeared more than 170 years ago on June 16, 1833, in *The Atlantic Journal* back in the "good old days!"

How can you avoid becoming a casualty of the "bad new days"? Take the offensive. Instead of "stewing" start "doing." Pay attention to the early warning signs of change. Look for changes in your industry, your family life, and your region. You cannot innovate if your understanding of change is misinformed, incomplete, or outdated.

Success in the new era is heavily dependent upon innovation, creativity, and problem-solving for which there are no precedents. While new technology is often the driver of economic and social change, the real opportunities are created by individuals who apply technology in new ways. Fred Smith, operating outside of the airline industry, created Federal Express because he saw the trend of speed in delivery of goods and services.

Your success depends on how well you think. Most of us are not paid to collect, sort, store, or retrieve information, although you do these things every day. You are paid to interpret that information and create and implement new ideas. Ask yourself:

- What can I offer that "they" aren't offering? Where's the niche that hasn't been developed? How can I add value to the service or products I promote?
- Where is the market inefficiency? What would make this process more convenient? How can I do this less expensively?
- What would people pay for that isn't available now?
- Which consumer groups and Internet communities are the most likely prospects for what I provide?

What trends will change my business and life? Think differently. Or as Billy G would say, take a Left on Red.

INDEX